W. L. DOW

JENNIFER DUMKE

W. L. DOW

The Architect Who Shaped Sioux Falls

THE History PRESS

Published by The History Press
Charleston, SC 29403
www.historypress.net

First published 2013

Manufactured in the United States

ISBN 978.1.62619.152.5

Library of Congress CIP data applied for.

Notice: The information in this book is true and complete to the best of our knowledge. It is offered without guarantee on the part of the author or The History Press. The author and The History Press disclaim all liability in connection with the use of this book.

I dedicate this book to my husband, Brad, who gave me the courage and confidence to take on such an endeavor. Along with our daughter, Kaydence, I couldn't be more proud of my family. Despite my love of the past, there's nothing more important than the present.

CONTENTS

FOREWORD

Each of our lives can be characterized as fabric, threads of different colors and strengths crossing and re-crossing one another to make cloth. Every person is different, and his or her stories make different and colorful cloth. Some people's stories will be collected, interpreted and permanently recorded. Other stories will be misplaced, and most will be lost. Those of us who enjoy looking back at history look for the bits and pieces or threads that can be woven together. We like weaving the threads together so we can understand the past and that which makes up our present.

It would not take a long time living in towns like Pipestone and Luverne, Minnesota, or Flandreau, Dell Rapids and Sioux Falls, South Dakota, to notice their pink stone buildings. Often these buildings have delicate features carved into the blocks of the rock that make sturdy, strong structures. Often one observes that these buildings have structural elements that carry from one building to another.

Here, Jennifer Dumke comes to the rescue. She was aware that a gentleman, Wallace Dow, an architect, had created some of these pretty pink structures. Where was the information about him? Where is the essential fabric that made up his life and work? Quickly she discovered that there were bits and pieces, short strings of information about Mr. Dow. Now, after many years of research, Mrs. Dumke has woven the fabric of Wallace Dow's life and work together for us to enjoy. He made many important contributions to the early architecture of Sioux Falls and this region. She has produced a book about his life that weaves the fibers together into colorful cloth.

Robert Kolbe
Local historian, former Minnehaha County commissioner and author of *They Captured the Moment*, a book on photographers of Dakota Territory

PREFACE

After many years of research and mounting curiosity, I'm proud to present to the community the life and works of a true architectural genius best known for his "pink palaces." Wallace Dow is considered the first true architect of Dakota Territory. His work dates back to 1880, when he first arrived in Yankton with his brother Wilbur. From that point on, Dow would go on to construct an insurmountable number of structures both in Sioux Falls and surrounding communities. Although many factors can be attributed to the success of early Sioux Falls, what Dow created were tangible symbols. Most people are familiar with his famed accomplishments, such as the penitentiary, the Pettigrew House and Museum and the Old Courthouse Museum, but most are unaware of the man behind the masonry.

In 2004, my husband and I took on the task of profiling Wallace Dow and his many works with the intent of producing a documentary. What we discovered was truly amazing. Not only were the buildings we knew of intricate and beautiful, but we also discovered countless other structures to which he lent his architectural skills. Some were modest, timber buildings that featured very little ornamentation. Others were grand and boasted his famed Richardsonian Romanesque style. We felt this said a lot about Dow as a person. Since very little is known about his personal life, we were forced to draw conclusions based on his career and the people he worked for. From that, it was clear this man should be recognized for his achievements.

In 2013, the documentary *W.L. Dow, Architect* debuted. Not knowing what type of interest the community would have, we took a chance and were overwhelmed by the response. We discovered interest on many levels; some knew of Dow but didn't know all his works, while others were in awe at the number of prominent buildings Dow was responsible for designing. This book takes our knowledge of Dow one step further. Not only does it include surrounding communities, but it also elaborates on Sioux Falls structures and even early prominent citizens. I hope that readers will enjoy and learn from this history and take pride in the structures that remain. Many are lost and some are in need of repair, while others are fully renovated and shine like new pennies. It's important to appreciate what Dow did for our community and make every effort possible to preserve his legacy for future generations.

ACKNOWLEDGEMENTS

In researching with my husband for the documentary *W.L. Dow, Architect*, I quickly realized that to make an interesting and accurate account of a local architect famed for his work over a century ago could not be done without the help of countless individuals. I was fortunate to have access to information, photographs and even homes as my husband and I embarked on our journey. It was an undertaking, but with the help of numerous communities, our dream to tell the story of Wallace Dow became a reality.

Even though much of the research had been compiled for the film, it was obvious much more was needed to write a book. In doing so, these acknowledgements include not only those who assisted with the recent book but also those who aided in producing our film.

First and foremost, I'd like to thank the Siouxland Heritage Museums for providing countless pictures and many hours of staff assistance to help verify information and locate images. Special consideration goes to Bill Hoskins, museum director, for paving the way. Other staff of the museum I'd like to recognize include Shelly Sjovold, collections assistant; Adam Nyhaug, museum registrar; Kevin Gansz, curator of education; and Staci Limoges, events coordinator.

In addition to the Siouxland Heritage Museums, I'd like to thank Robert Kolbe for lending his writing abilities for the foreword of this book and for his valuable insight and recommendations. Kolbe, a local historian, former Minnehaha County commissioner and author of *They Captured the Moment*, a book on photographers of Dakota Territory, also provided images from his private collection called Robert Kolbe Dakota Collection. My husband and I spent many enjoyable hours at his personal residence scanning his expansive stereograph collection and learning more about Dakota Territory history.

Special thanks go out to the numerous local authors who share my passion for history and have provided information on many of Dow's structures. Special thanks to Wayne Fanebust, author of *Where the Sioux River Bends*; David Erpestad and David Wood, authors of *Building South Dakota: A Historical Survey of the State's Architecture to 1945*; and Gary D. Olson and Erik Olson, authors of *Sioux Falls, South Dakota: A Pictorial History*. Other individuals who have aided me in my first writing venture include Erik Renshaw, author of *Forgotten Sioux Falls*, and Tom Dempster, author of *North of Twelfth Street*.

There are many others to thank for helping to make this companion book to the documentary possible. Thank you to our interviewees, Bill Hoskins, Gary Olson, Robert Kolbe, Wayne Fanebust, Carol Mashek, Jeff Hazard, David Erpestad, Dave Farrar and Mary Glenski. Special consideration must be given to the staff at the South Dakota State Historical Society, specifically Liz Almlie, SE historic preservation specialist, for their assistance in our initial project. Others to be noted include Angie Rabon, Brenda Rustad, Catherine Wagner, Ted and Karen Muenster, Marcy Bird, Susan Hoskins, Anne Larsen, Debra Giatkowski, Vernon Brown, Mike Cooper, Crystal Nelson, Susan Kudera, Dan Daily, Sarah Hanson, Colleen Bents, the Historic Dayton House Board of Directors, the City of Sioux Falls, the Minnehaha County Historical Society, the Siouxland Heritage Museum Alliance and the Sioux Falls Board of Historic Preservation.

Another area of support that I encountered when releasing *W.L. Dow, Architect* was the local media and all the fans of the film. Without their intentions, the community would never have been exposed to our efforts and this book would not have been possible. Thank you to KELO TV, KSFY TV, the *Rick Knobe Radio Show*, South Dakota Public Radio, the *Argus Leader*, *Clear Lake Courier*, *South Dakota Magazine*, *Sioux Falls Woman Magazine*, *Yankton Press & Dakotan*, the *Worthington Daily Globe* and the various local newsletters and community calendars. A special thank-you to South Dakota Public Broadcasting, specifically Bob Bosse, director of television, for accepting our film and promoting it on a national level.

I would especially like to thank the Dow family for their participation in *W.L. Dow, Architect* and for their pending anticipation of this book. Without them, Dow's legacy would most certainly have been lost. It is with great pleasure that I gained additional insight into the man through his extended family. Some even provided memorabilia and images never seen before. Although this book is to honor and remember Wallace Dow for his work, it's also a tribute to his family, with whom he shared many similar traits and qualities.

This book would never have been possible without the communities on which Dow made an impact. From homeowners to businesses, city officials to nonprofits, the legacy of Wallace Dow lives on in many of his restored structures. Although tribute must be paid to those for whom the wrecking ball or fire led to their demise, it's with great pride that numerous communities treasure the work left standing. Thank you to Rod Evans, owner of Evans Photography located in the Law Exchange Block, for taking my photograph and restoring one of Dow's most impressive downtown structures.

Finally, special appreciation goes out to all those who have allowed me the time to invest in writing this book. To my husband, Brad, for assisting with the images and providing support, and to my co-workers at the Avera McKennan Foundation, specifically W. Tim Kromminga, for giving me the time and encouragement to take on such an endeavor. Without all of you, I would never have been able to accomplish this milestone in my life.

I hope that the readers will find as much pleasure in this book as I have found in researching and writing it. It was with great aspiration that I was able to acknowledge all of Dow's work, but as mentioned in the introduction, many believe Dow's work is not confined to the working list of structures we go by today. I believe Dow had a much broader impact that we will continue to learn more about as more buildings and information surface. But for now, we must treasure what we have and leave the unknown in our dreams.

INTRODUCTION

During a time when land was "free" and business deals were made on a handshake, the early days of Dakota Territory can best be described as naïve optimism. Only a few brave prospectors and soldiers weathered the rough winters in the 1850s, but the sparkle of the cascading falls of the Big Sioux River in their eyes kept dreams alive. These men didn't have a crystal ball. They had the promise of water power with the rushing waters of the Big Sioux River and quarrying with the vast abundance of pink quartzite to skew their futures. What the handful of men didn't anticipate were the years of harsh winters and brutal attacks chipping away at them. With dwindling numbers, the few who remained on the land lived in crude shelters and barracks. It was a roof over their heads and that was about all. But the winds of change were beginning to blow.

The city of Sioux Falls gradually became a reality by the 1870s, thanks to the pioneering efforts of these early frontiersman and prospectors. Life was still hard. They knew they needed something to attract more easterners to uproot and make the venture. That something was reassurance. And one man had the talents to grant it. It would be a gentleman from New Hampshire named Wallace Dow who would literally shape the city of Sioux Falls. Not found in his pocketbook or business aspirations, Dow offered reassurance during a time of uncertainty through architectural design. Although his buildings have lasted throughout history, his name has been forgotten. His famed Minnehaha County Courthouse pierces the sky with its 165-foot clock tower; meanwhile, his gravestone is no bigger than a briefcase.

Dow arrived in Dakota Territory with his brother in 1880. The catalyst for this decision remains unknown; however, many theories exist. Upon his arrival, the city of Sioux Falls and its surrounding townships were nothing to write home about. Mostly small shanty sod homes and structures with false fronts dotted the dirt streets. But the city had a buried secret. Below the surface was a layer of quartzite three feet in depth that ran from eastern Dakota Territory all the way to Minnesota. Gigantic outcroppings created the wondrous cascades of the falls, while other smaller ones barely peeked above the surface. This mineral resource gave life to Dow's architectural creations. His mission to build reassurance through sturdy and strong structures succeeded at giving the illusion of a city that was going places.

Dow began building in 1880, and he virtually never stopped. As he built more structures, each would stretch the design limits a bit more. A little taller here, maybe additional arches there—his work was a unique culmination of the famed Romanesque design paired with a twist of his own personal style.

Dow's designs were true masterpieces. He moved away from the rationale of reassurance and began building decadence. Wealthy citizens didn't blink an eye at doling out large sums of money for extravagant homes. Bold archways, larger-than-life turrets and loud colors were his livelihood during the Victorian era. But the same descriptions—bold and loud—were the polar opposite of Dow's personality as a humble architect in Dakota Territory.

Sioux Falls prospered, and the commissions continued to roll in. His humble nature and quiet demeanor were regarded as favorable but may have been part of the mystery surrounding Wallace Dow today. Over time, the lack of knowledge and information on Wallace Dow allowed his name to virtually disappear. Urban culture and the wrecking ball were the demise of many of his famous structures. Today, while many mourn the loss of some of the city's most breathtaking structures, respect and tribute are paid to those restored and still standing. Even though his name has melted away, some believe it's the way Dow would have wanted it—to be remembered for his buildings rather than himself.

Chapter 1

EARLY DAYS OF DAKOTA TERRITORY

The year was 1856, and what was to be Dakota Territory lay patiently waiting even though the rumblings of competition could be heard in the far distance. Two rival land companies were making their way to the serene grasslands of what was then called the American West. It wasn't just the early accounts and publications from pioneers who described the fertile soils with such eagerness that drew the attention of those willing to tame the uncontrolled land. It was the lure of something much bigger, much more powerful and unique to the area that led men to risk everything to make the trip and stake claim. That something was the falls of the Big Sioux River. It acted as a magnet, with pink stone outcroppings and rushing waters violently cascading into a lazy basin where the waters were eased back again into the mundane river flow.

Imaginations ran wild, and speculators arrived to find the accounts were true. The iconic falls were just as breathtaking and powerful, the land was just as fertile, the grasses were just as high and the struggle would be just as backbreaking. Two separate companies—the Dakota Land Company from St. Paul, Minnesota, and the Western Town Company from Dubuque, Iowa—quickly organized and took up 320 acres along the falls under federal law for town sites. The Western Town Company and its group of prospectors were the first to arrive. Although they were separate companies, they didn't hesitate to put rivalry aside due to the harsh conditions and the need for protection. The Western Town Company quickly constructed a log cabin on a small island located by the falls of the Big Sioux River, which marked the beginning of a township.

Over the next five years, sickness, violent attacks and brutal winters chipped away at what few land speculators remained. In 1861, President James Buchanan signed the Organic Act, creating Dakota Territory. The federal census at the time listed a mere forty-two people. But it was the signing of the Homestead Act the next year that caused a flurry of easterners to flock to what was referred to as the "land of opportunity." The act provided that a settler could claim 160 acres with stipulations that he was to live on it for five years, make improvements, cultivate the land and even build a home. If all requirements were met, the land was his to keep.

Cries of "free land" were heard around the country, yet only a precious few could meet the criteria. The Civil War had an impact both nationally and in Dakota Territory. Most homesteaders waited for the hostility to end before making such a journey. But it didn't last long. The year 1866 marked the onset of what was to be called the first Dakota land boom. Early arrivers had the opportunity to cherry-pick the areas with the most fertile soils and best access to water and trees. Later, settlers found all land located along the river had been acquired. It was official: what once was referred to as uninhabited prairie grasses had officially become an agricultural region.

By the 1870s, Sioux Falls had undergone many transformations. Life was hard for those who weathered frigid winters and acts of nature beyond comprehension. Yet the potential for prosperity kept Sioux Falls on the radar for both prominent and humble pioneers. Beauty aside, it was a natural mineral resource of pink quartzite rock that had many seeing green. This glacier-made stone was three hundred feet deep with outcroppings that ran primarily between Dakota Territory and Minnesota. Like little hints of what lies beneath, Minnesota had already developed profitable quarrying industries. Soon, all eyes focused on the falls. Known for its hardness, geologists named the stone Sioux quartzite, but it was also referred to as Jasper, Rose Quartz and Sioux Falls Granite. The bedrock of pink stone was inexhaustible, and its outcroppings provided ample potential for quarrying. Prominent speculators viewed Sioux Falls like a best-kept secret they could now shout from the mountaintops. Visions of settlers flocking to the budding city soon became reality.

The settlers looked to the land to construct the first stone hotel, called the Dubuque House, in 1857. Mostly crude in nature and hardly deserving of being called "architecture," Sioux Falls had its first hotel. The primitive hotel was recalled as being built of undressed blocks of pink quartzite found along the falls. Although no actual images exist, early speculation describes it as a simple rectangle featuring a single room with a loft above and cellar below. Guests more than likely slept on cloth sack mattresses filled with the same prairie grasses that surrounded them. The Dubuque House served its purpose and would play a vital part in developing what was later called the "Queen City."

Later, Fort Dakota was developed and a stone commissary was built in the late 1860s. But it wasn't until 1872 that the first quarry was recorded: the George Boardman quarry.

Sioux Falls and its native quartzite were gaining notoriety. Still, weathered timber homes and stores with large false fronts dotted the landscape and sat prone to prairie fires. The grandiose potential of Sioux quartzite needed refinement. It needed the expertise of skilled laborers to expose the true potential for this natural resource that would become a symbol of pride and profit. It also needed the skill of an architect who could design iconic structures out of the stone. Both were soon to occur.

Years before Dow arrived in Dakota Territory, early pioneers had already tapped into harnessing water power and were utilizing native quartzite as a building material. Unfortunately, promoters and investors seeking to save money on construction by quarrying near the building site were suddenly eyeing the rushing waters that had shrined the falls for beauty. With water power a big opportunity, plans for flour mills located along the forceful cascades began to develop. Then the quarrying began. Initially, the stair-step falls themselves were quarried to construct the mills in addition to other building projects around the city. No one could comprehend the irreversible damage that was being done to an earthly wonder but, rather, interpreted its existence as a way to live off the land.

Basements for both the Sioux Falls Mill in 1873 and the Cascade Mill in 1877 were constructed from the very quartzite they rested on. It wasn't until 1879 that a seven-story structure was built along the falls, becoming the first large building to use the abundant and beautiful resource. It was called the Queen Bee Mill. All three mills harnessed the rushing cascades of the Big Sioux River as a source of water power to create pounds and pounds of flour. In fact, the Queen Bee superstructure produced as much as one hundred barrels of flour a day. Between its quartzite basement story, water-harnessed energy source and native timber wood-framed roof, the Queen Bee was one of the best examples of using what was available to make money.

The concept of building such industrial structures near what was supposed to be reserved as a local attraction or park area created frenzy.

An early quarry in Sioux Falls. Pioneers immediately took advantage of the native stone and its potential to build homes and pave roads. *Siouxland Heritage Museums.*

Even though local capitalists urged such measures be taken, the public outcry turned political. The idea of a train depot being constructed near the falls had even been objected to. Despite it all, the Queen Bee and its long list of salivating investors prevailed, and citizens watched barrel upon barrel of flour be hauled out on horse and buggy. It didn't take long for many to realize the supersized mistake the Queen Bee Mill had been.

As water power slowed down due to the occasional droughts, profits slowed down even more. Eastern investors began to research the feasibility of such a structure, questioning whether local capitalists were looking to create a seven-story wonder that used local resources to gain population rather than create a sustainable business. Soon the mill was forced to shut down. And while the rushing waters were left unharmed, measurable damage had been done to the quartzite cascades and the landscape of what was considered the city's finest example of unique beauty. The only positive conclusion that could be drawn was the ability to use native quartzite to create such a wondrous structure, even if it did forever obstruct the nature views of the area.

In the end, one might say the falls had the last laugh. Over the next thirty years, the mill would close and reopen several times. Sporadic newspaper headlines would boast of the spark investors would ignite to get the mill producing again. But they all failed. The skyscraper that tore into the cascades was thought to forever stand as a large symbol of arrogance and eagerness to sell a city despite the costs.

In 1956, a large fire claimed the uninhabited structure, which was being used as a warehouse. The one-time seven-story building had been filed down to a mere one-story area of ruins, restoring the beautiful views of the park.

Despite the controversy, no one could argue that the Queen Bee had in fact been constructed of native Sioux quartzite. By the year 1879, a number of stone buildings began to occupy Sioux Falls. Local Sioux Falls booster E.A. Sherman used stone to build a number of his projects, and that was just the beginning. Crude as they were, promoters knew they needed skill to use this invaluable resource to its full potential, and it was likely this talent wouldn't come from Dakota Territory. Regional newspapers began to tout the stone industry to lure skilled masons to bring their talents to shape and mold the stone. They also knew these masons had families and would be tempted to start a new life in Dakota Territory. Word spread, and stonecutters were recruited from as far away as England. With chisel in hand, each skilled laborer knew exactly where to strike a stone to make a perfect cut. As the number of stonecutters grew, so did the number of quarries. It was to mark the beginning of something beautiful.

Chapter 2

Growing Up in the Granite State

Across the map, things were quite different for young Wallace Leroy Dow. Born in 1844 in Croydon, New Hampshire, to Hial and Laura Dow, the young boy took to his father's trade of woodworking and received his formal education at the Powers Institute at Bernardston, Massachusetts. While most men of his generation ended up fighting in the Civil War, Dow was spared. It has been cited that the War Department did engage Dow in secret work, but nothing was confirmed. Dow focused his energies on architecture and devoted several years working in the heating and plumbing business in Springfield, Massachusetts. Here he gained such valuable knowledge that upon returning to New Hampshire, he quickly organized the firm of W.L. Dow & Company. He was only twenty-two years old, and already Dow had built an extensive enterprise that would continue for several years. In 1870, Dow also became partner with his father in a firm called H. & W.L. Dow.

Having been bred from a family with deep roots in the building and carpentry industry, Dow had a specific interest in architecture. And he had the perfect mentor to lead him to greatness. His uncle Edward Dow was a prominent architect in the state of New Hampshire. From 1877 until he moved to Dakota Territory in 1880, Dow studied under his influence, gaining invaluable knowledge of architecture in a land referred to as the "Granite State."

Like the pink hues of native Sioux quartzite, New Hampshire bore a similar stone resource called granite and was quite advanced when it came to utilizing

Young Wallace Dow and his brother Wilbur arrived in Yankton in 1880. *Siouxland Heritage Museums.*

the stone to its full potential. Dating back to the colonial times, easterners used what they called split and dimensional stone for foundations, wells and cobbles. Like quartzite, granite also varied in color and grain, making certain quarries, most likely those near a water source, more desirable. As the industry grew, inland granite eventually became a popular choice as a main building material and went on to be used for decades, proving both profitable and impressive in looks.

Edward Dow frequently incorporated the use of native granite in his grand designs. His impressive building résumé included such significant structures as the Charleston Town Hall, the Memorial Arch of Tilton and the St. Paul Episcopal Church in Concord, which today is still regarded as one of the state's best Gothic Revival buildings. A local newspaper serving both Newport and Charleston referred to Edward Dow as the "Prince of Architects." But it was the New Hampshire State Penitentiary, built in 1878, that gave young Wallace direct exposure to constructing such an intricate public institution.

Legislation had just been passed providing approval for the erection of a new state prison. The cost was not to exceed $200,000, with specifications that it be large enough to house two hundred convicts. This bid included all the necessary offices and workshops as well. Ground was broken in 1878, and funding was allotted for additional cells. Work commenced in 1880, the same year Wallace departed for Dakota Territory. It's not known whether Wallace ever saw the prison, which was described by local newspapers as one of the best-built and most convenient prisons of the modern world open for operation. And while some would claim that Wallace Dow was self-taught and inventive, these symbolic structures proved he did in fact have a solid education and studied under a successful architect whose bloodline he shared.

While at work, young Dow spent his days designing massive structures alongside his famous uncle. But at home, his first project was a modest personal residence in Newport, New Hampshire. The simplistic and small house was located on Summer Street and provided a home for his wife, Lois, and their many children. Known for being a family man, the Dow family faced many tragedies. Before moving to Dakota Territory, the Dows already had lost three children, the youngest being seven-month-old Jessie, who was buried the very year Wallace left. Two years later, they welcomed daughter Annie. She would be the family's first true native of South Dakota.

In 1880, Wallace Dow made the decision to uproot and make the journey to Dakota Territory while his family remained in New Hampshire. The exact reason behind such an enormous decision remains unknown, although many theories do exist. The country had faced a severe economic recession during the 1870s, and Dow's personal business may have been a casualty. Others believe he was adventuresome and saw potential in Dakota Territory, joining many other East Coast pioneers and speculators looking to acquire land and a new life. But the most likely theory remains that of a controversial governor who many believe had specifically recruited Dow and solicited his move to the West.

Nehemiah G. Ordway served as territorial governor of Dakota Territory from 1880 to 1884. Ranking as one of the territory's most controversial governors, Ordway was often charged with flagrant excesses of authority and political patronage. He was also a native of New Hampshire, where the banks held a considerable amount of investments in Dakota land. A member of the New Hampshire legislature, he was sponsored for his position as governor of Dakota by that body. In May 1880, he was officially elected governor of Dakota Territory. Within a mere six months, Ordway had appointed Dow, a young and unknown architect, to the board of directors for a newly created territorial penitentiary in Sioux Falls. While Dow would not receive any form of compensation for holding this position, it did provide funding for fees and expenses to relocate. This may have been the golden ticket for Dow to travel west, where he had the potential to dominate the construction world of the new Dakota Territory.

Accompanied by his brother Wilbur Dow, thirty-six-year-old Wallace arrived in the town of Pierre three weeks before the first railroad train. It was quickly realized that Pierre was not a bustling place, and within a year, the Dow brothers moved to Yankton, which served as the territorial capital at the time. The territory was in the midst of an economic boom, and Dow was quickly put to work. The penitentiary board quickly appointed W.L. Dow to provide the plans and specifications for the penitentiary. It was Dow's first architectural commission in the new land. Thankfully, his talents to create history-making, symbolic structures would dwarf the speculations of his relocation to Dakota Territory.

Chapter 3

THE BEGINNING OF A LEGACY

Located on a high bluff overlooking the wondrous falls of the Big Sioux River, the Dakota Territorial Penitentiary would be the first of many Dow-designed public institutions. Not hesitating to utilize the native abundance of Sioux quartzite, the prisoners themselves quarried the stone used to construct the massive structure rather than the skilled masons Dow would later employ. Although the prisoners were not formally trained, it was said that only those skilled enough to properly cut stone were used. The building was described as a unique work of architecture that spanned the styles of Italianate and Second Empire. Cellblocks with windows that ran several stories high flanked a central, multiuse building. Later, a massive quartzite wall would be erected in addition to a water tower. The warden's house, designed by Dow using a combination of Italianate and Second Empire features, was added to the front in 1884.

This project was Dow making a name for himself and proving his skills as a qualified architect. His second big commission would prove even more impressive and forward thinking. The nineteenth century saw considerable growth in state-sponsored treatment of the mentally ill in the United States, and the rise of asylum building became a necessity. Since Dakota Territory was in its embryotic stage in 1875, the first mentally ill patients were housed in St. Peter, Minnesota. Although the census indicated anywhere from seven patients to thirteen, the territory was paying a hefty sum of $5 per week for their care out of state. In 1878, William Howard of Michigan became Dakota Territory's first governor and was called upon to build a local home

The Dakota Territorial Penitentiary, built in 1880, was Dow's first commission and already demonstrated his love of native quartzite. In 1884, the water tower, warden's house and massive wall surrounding the penitentiary were added. *Siouxland Heritage Museums.*

for the insane. The first hospital was made of reclaimed wood, and although no pictures exist, it's recorded that Governor Howard paid just over $2,000 from his private funds to construct a main hospital and one wing.

The corridors quickly filled up with local patients. The territory was saving money, but it was doing so at a high cost. The rustic buildings were quickly deemed unsafe because of their combustible character. In 1881, Dow received $370 for the plans to construct a much grander hospital for the insane in Yankton. But before the construction was complete, fire broke out in the first wooden structure, and it was burned to the ground, killing five patients in a mere thirty minutes. Fortunately, Dow was already hard at work creating a new and permanent hospital building to house the seventy patients in the first wooden framed structure. It was to be majestic in nature and safe for its patients. Heated with stoves and lit with kerosene lamps, the project was overseen by Dr. S.B. McGlumphy at a cost of $75,000. Dow, having done much research on mental institutions, quickly adapted his design to employ an arrangement made popular in the 1850s called the Linear Kirkbride Plan.

Dr. Thomas Story Kirkbride was an advocate for creating an asylum system based on the tenets of moral treatment and promoted a set of detailed building principles that influenced the construction and operation of many American asylums built during this period. One of these would be

Dow's Yankton Territorial Hospital for the Insane. Kirkbride viewed patients as active participants in therapy, with the buildings and their surroundings acting as central components of treatment. His linear plan was based on hierarchical segregation of residents according to symptoms and even sex. The wings were subdivided, with more severe cases farther away from the administration building and the less severe on the upper levels closer to the center. The idea was to make the patients' experience more comfortable by isolating them from others with different symptoms. In addition to linear buildings, Kirkbride's design also called for fireproof construction, acres of surrounding farmland and landscaped grounds. Kirkbride believed access to fresh air and sunlight was vital in treatment. Dow followed those guidelines and designed a striking hospital to serve the community.

Unlike the other structures, the Laundry Cottage was a two-story granite structure that was designed by Dow mainly for service and to occupy staff housing. Due to increasing patient numbers and declining funds for additional buildings, patients were housed on the second level of the stone structure, which forced the staff to take up residence in the attic. The building was heated by steam heat, with one stove in the basement used solely for heating flat irons. Nearly twenty years after its initial construction by Wallace Dow, occupants of the building were awakened by dense smoke. There were over sixty staff and patients occupying the Laundry Cottage when a fire broke out, killing seventeen patients who couldn't escape due to their conditions. As was common at the time, a campus cemetery was included in the asylum construction. But the manner in which the hospital recognized the seventeen patients who perished was quite unusual and created a number of folklore stories that would forever haunt the campus. Seventeen rectangle stones bearing only a patient number were arranged in the form of a cross and placed in the ground with no other identifying information.

Eventually, the buildings that composed the Kirkbride Plan were either destroyed by fire or deterioration or were razed one by one. The Kirkbride Plan itself lost prominence in the system, and therefore, many of Dow's original plans were not rebuilt according to this concept. A lack of concrete evidence that substantial numbers of patients were permanently cured forced the mental healthcare establishment to seek different forms of treatment. Noteworthy for his efforts, Dr. Kirkbride still helped many patients even though a new generation of asylum superintendents began advocating different forms of designs based on different concepts of care. Soon the Kirkbride Plan became obsolete.

For Dow, his once grand and forward-thinking campus quickly adopted the "cottage plan" and began to employ various architects for ongoing work. Today, only the Lee Cottage and the Carriage House remain as testaments to Dow's work. Abandoning concrete, Dow's Lee Cottage is known for its rusticated appearance, created by using quarry-faced cut quartzite stone laid in a random ashlar pattern. Possibly an introduction to his Romanesque style, the two-and-a-half-story rectangle building was impressive with Kasota limestone belt courses and a gable roof. The structure now sits vacant but still stands today as a testament to Dow's influence on the campus.

Despite the crumbling walls and fires at the Yankton Territorial Hospital for the Insane, it was still a major endeavor. The growing population put demands on proper housing for the poor as well. As an act of community service, Dow was commissioned to construct the Minnehaha County Poor House located north of Sioux Falls. The board for the Minnehaha County Poor House inspected a number of government and pauper relief systems. After close review, the county chose to adopt what was known as the Milwaukee System for the new poorhouse.

The Milwaukee System had been in place since 1852 and originated at Almshouse Poor House in Milwaukee. The system required two things for

The Lee Cottage, located at the Dakota Territorial Hospital for the Insane in Yankton, is one of the few remaining structures of Dow's original plan for the hospital. *Human Services Center.*

admission: a judge's order to document poverty and a lack of any relatives and friends; and the signature of two county taxpayers. Although it is not clear exactly how closely the Minnehaha County Poor House followed the Milwaukee System, the Almshouse Poor House even admitted disabled individuals and alcoholics. For Dow, this meant constructing a building meant solely for purpose. A high contrast to the Dakota Territorial Hospital, Dow's design was vaguely Greek Revival but did demonstrate his willingness to handle small projects as well as large. Eventually, the buildings were razed, leaving a single structure that sat abandoned. For years, it remained on a horse ranch until finally being razed.

Back in Sioux Falls, the city was experiencing growth. In 1870, the city had a population of 5 people. By 1880, the city had grown to over 2,100 residents and was officially chartered three years later, making Sioux Falls a city rather than a village. Dow was getting more commissions in Sioux Falls, and when the territory capital was moved to Bismarck in 1883, he moved his office and family to Sioux Falls. Being the resident architect, Dow was quickly commissioned to construct a nearly replica of the Dakota Territorial Penitentiary in the new capital. Distinctive features of this prison include heavy Italianate window moldings of light-colored Kasota stone, which provided a unique contrast to the red quartzite walls.

Although Bismarck would only remain the territory capital until statehood was achieved in 1889, Dow did a small number of commissions in the area. One was a personal residence for C.W. Thompson. Thompson was a resident expert in the mining and handling of what was called Dakota coal, another abundant natural resource of Dakota Territory. Like quartzite was to Sioux Falls and granite was to New Hampshire, the northern portion of Dakota Territory had an abundance of lignite coal, which also cropped out in many places. Although not a building material for Dow to utilize in his design for the Thompson House, it did provide for excellent heating and gas-making qualities superior to almost any coal discovered on the continent. Thompson capitalized on this resource and gained wealth from his knowledge of the material.

Dow's next commission up north was the First Presbyterian Church. In 1873, a Presbyterian church in Bismarck was the first church to be organized in what is now North Dakota. Early accounts say the church was operated out of a tent until 1885, when more structured churches were being built.

Just as Bismarck was taking shape, Sioux Falls was on its heels. Dow was in demand, and as the only architect, he was the logical choice for many local business owners and residents. Still not very impressive, the city was now a hybrid of shanty one-story wood buildings and unimpressive stone structures and homes. But as the quarry industry began to take shape in the 1880s, more substantial structures reflecting Dow's vision soon sprouted from the prairie soils.

One of the driving forces behind Dow's legacy was the ability to utilize creativity in design. To do this, he needed paying customers willing to spend the money for such lavish projects. Sioux Falls at the time experienced a dichotomy of life. While some lived in striking Victorian homes, others bunked with their oxen. National trends were beginning to improve, but Sioux Falls had a far more unique way of gaining prosperity and notoriety.

Beginning in the 1880s, an honest oversight in legislature would result in one of the most controversial yet successful decades of all time. A liberal ninety-day residency law, and the testimony of local judges that a legal divorce could be obtained, spread like wildfire across the United States. As a result, Sioux Falls instantly became known as the "divorce capital." It was said that thousands of people with wedlock woes scurried into town to seek legal separation from their spouses. The result was a staggering divorce rate in Minnehaha County. In fact, it was three times that of the entire United States during that period. Local residents grew displeased with the shamed fame Sioux Falls was receiving. Eventually, divorce laws were tightened after South Dakota achieved statehood in 1889, and Sioux Falls was stripped of its reference as the divorce capital by the early 1900s. But one couldn't argue that it was the surge of "tourists" that necessitated the construction of a number of new hotels and restaurants.

One of the most well-known hotels was the infamous Cataract House. In 1871, Harry Corson moved to Dakota Territory from his native state of Maine after hearing of the opportunities available in Sioux Falls. Already engaged in the hotel industry, he quickly began constructing the Cataract House, fittingly named after the rushing cascades of the falls. In 1878, his brother Henry joined him, and they operated under the name of W.H. Corson & Brother.

The brothers were hotel tycoons, as they soon went on to make extensive additions and remodeled the building due to a need for additional capacity. The early structure was not impressive in looks but was still the most popular hotel in the area. It was said that Harry not only was "born in a hotel, but knew how to keep a hotel." The Cataract House was the first hotel built in Minnehaha County that had reasonable facilities to accommodate the traveling public.

By 1881, the team of brothers employed Dow to build a much grander structure that stood on the corner of Ninth Street and Phillips Avenue. Bearing the same name, the original hotel needed to be moved out into Ninth Street during construction so business could continue. It was the central location for news and business in Sioux Falls but also served as a place for local business

Left: The Cataract House, built for the Corson brothers, was one of the finest places to stay in Sioux Falls. Advertisements frequently touted the structure as it gained notoriety from all over. *Siouxland Heritage Museums.*

Below: Standing on the corner of Ninth Street and Phillips Avenue, the Cataract House was popular for social gatherings and was often the choice meeting place for city officials and business owners. Its Second Empire style made for a grand appearance that was alluring to both tourists and local residents. *Siouxland Heritage Museums.*

leaders to discuss plans for the new city. It even was the starting point for the city's street-numbering system, which is still in use today. Although Dow was never a master of the Second Empire style, the characteristic mansard roof was a fine showcase of Dow's commercial capabilities. The new fortress was brick and employed a bevy of local building materials and an observation tower. It was the city's finest place to stay and also housed the finest place to eat—a true tribute to the Corson brothers who ran it.

The Commercial House, built in 1883, was constructed using part of another building that was moved from Main Avenue. Dow used a simple style and chose pressed brick over quartzite. *Siouxland Heritage Museums.*

Although some would say the hotel was bursting from bustling tourists, which was partially true, it was actually unhappy husbands and wives that drove the need to expand hotel accommodations. It was quite obvious that local residents scoffed at those residing in town merely to wait out their time for a divorce, but for the merchants, politicians and especially lawyers, it was their bread and butter. They relied on the deep pockets of desperate easterners to sustain their expensive lifestyles and continue growing the small city.

Advertising steam heat, electric light and rates of $2 per day, Dow's Commercial House in 1883 soon gave a bit of competition to the Cataract House. The original Commercial House, built for William E. Willey in 1878, was constructed using part of another building that was moved from Main Avenue to form the north half of the building. The original house stood for only five years before fire soon claimed this structure and Willey enlisted Dow's talents for the new Commercial House. Not nearly as grand in nature, Dow demonstrated his loyalty to the city rather than the Corson brothers when he designed the four-story Italianate-style hotel also located on Phillips Avenue. At a cost of $40,000, Dow's plan called for a seventy- by one-hundred-foot building that would accommodate one hundred sleeping rooms. A simple design that utilized pressed brick, this hotel also faced early demise by fire the same year it was built. Willey rebuilt and sold the structure in 1885, and it would operate under several names, including the Teton and Anderson Hotel, before being razed in 1939 to build the Hollywood Theater.

Chapter 4

EARLY LEADERS AND INFLUENCES

Dow was well established and gained the trust of many prominent business leaders in Sioux Falls. Under the wing of the famed Sioux Falls businessman R.F. Pettigrew, Dow was first introduced to Bishop William Hare, which would mark the beginning of a long and prosperous relationship. Between the increased demand and support from these prominent citizens, Dow was catapulted as the territory's resident architect—although one would argue the competition at the time was none too fierce. Newspapers began to see advertisements bearing the infamous legend "W.L. Dow, Architect, Sioux Falls, Dakota." The list of buildings below his name was increasing, reaffirming what most could see just by taking a leisurely stroll around town. Dow was responsible for designing and shaping the landscape thanks to the savvy businessmen and city leaders who were also responsible for such success.

R.F. Pettigrew moved to Dakota Territory in 1869 to work as deputy surveyor and quickly settled and began practicing law. He was heavily into politics and was a member of the territorial House of Representatives. He was a driving force behind achieving statehood and promoting Sioux Falls at any cost. In fact, some of early antics cost him dearly, but most credit Pettigrew's achievements for stimulating the economy and promoting an up-and-coming city. He was elected as Republican to the U.S. House, serving from 1881 to 1883. He suffered losses and opposition, but most remember Pettigrew as a risk taker who was eager to serve the community. In 1889, South Dakota was admitted as a state and Pettigrew was elected as South

Above: Although Dow was one of few architects during the time, he still made a point to advertise in the local newspaper. Citizens were beginning to recognize his name and took note of his elegant structures. *Siouxland Heritage Museums.*

Left: R.F. Pettigrew was a politician and business owner. He is remembered as a driving force behind South Dakota achieving statehood and the overall success of Sioux Falls. He collaborated with Wallace Dow on numerous projects. *Siouxland Heritage Museums.*

Dakota's first senator to the United States, a position that he would fill until 1901. With his business partner, judge S.L. Tate, he formed the real estate firm Pettigrew and Tate. Together, they would donate more land to Sioux Falls than any other during that time. Pettigrew took to Dow's designs and visions to help fulfill his dreams. He even introduced a bill to fund structures with specifications that only native Sioux quartzite be used for the construction. Upon leaving the Senate, Pettigrew remained active in politics until his passing in 1926. He willed his home, which was designed by W.L. Dow in 1889, to the City of Sioux Falls. An amateur archaeologist, Pettigrew constructed an addition to his home to house his many artifacts. Today, the Pettigrew House and Museum has been restored and serves as a museum for the community to enjoy.

The relationship between Dow and Bishop Hare was quite different but equally as prosperous. Hare was an American bishop of the Protestant Episcopal Church. Born in New Jersey, he preached in Philadelphia and eventually made his way to Dakota Territory in 1883, when his diocese was extended. Known as a leading missionary in America, he was often called the "Apostle of the West" for his efforts in the Dakotas among both pioneers and Native Americans. In addition to being a dedicated missionary, Hare was credited with building one of the first educational institutions in Sioux Falls, called the All Saints School. Although it was not profitable, Hare continued to overlook any financial woes and focused on educating the community. During his final years, Hare became ill and fought a courageous battle until he passed away in Atlantic City in 1909. Just like Pettigrew, Hare's legacy and impact on the community lives on. All Saints School was forced to close, but Dow's work of art and Hare's mission stand tall today. Some of the original buildings have been fully restored and converted into a functional retirement facility.

After statehood had been achieved, another man would contribute to the success of South Dakota and provide Dow with handsome commissions. Andrew Carnegie was an industrialist and philanthropist who believed the public library was the greatest benefit one could provide for the community. Between 1897 and 1917, he provided the most abundant stimulus for the construction of free public libraries in South Dakota and the entire nation. His gifts exceeded $40 million, and over 1,600 libraries were constructed through his generous gifts to the community. Born in Scotland, Carnegie moved to the United States in 1848 and started work as a telegrapher. By the 1860s, he held numerous investments in the railroad industry and oil derricks. Additional success was achieved when he became a bond salesman, raising money for the American enterprise in Europe. His first company was Pittsburgh's Carnegie Steel Company, which he eventually sold to J.P. Morgan in 1901 for a reported $480 million. Having achieved such great success, Carnegie devoted the rest of his life to philanthropy and had a special interest in the development of local libraries. He also supported world peace, education and scientific research, but most remember him as being the "father of the library system," a title that would directly benefit numerous cities in South Dakota. His grants to certain cities specified that a suitable site must be acquired and that the library must maintain a free service at a minimum cost per year. In South Dakota, numerous towns such as Pierre, Yankton and Mitchell were awarded grants to construct Carnegie libraries, and Wallace Dow would provide the designs.

Bishop Hare shown with his students at the All Saints School that Dow built. Hare was often called the "Apostle of the West" for his efforts in the Dakotas. *Siouxland Heritage Museums.*

Early leaders such as R.F. Pettigrew and Bishop Hare were among the first to boost Dow's early career in Dakota Territory, and philanthropists such as Carnegie provided handsome commissions, but it was one man who went on to be known nationally to whom Dow would lend his talents: George Draper Dayton. Dayton arrived in Worthington, Minnesota, in the 1880s to lead a recovery effort for a poorly performing investment group in his native home of New York. Having acquired early success, he went on to be a banker and real estate developer in Worthington. Dayton was president of the Bank of Worthington and founded the Loan and Investment Company. He believed in living by religious principles by improving the community and served on numerous community boards. Dayton had great respect for Wallace Dow and commissioned a large family home to be built by him. Spanning eight lots, Dow designed a grand Georgian/Colonial Revival home with exquisite detailing and family-friendly amenities. The classic design included cedar shingles, large pediment dormers, a widow's walk and three chimneys. Dow made sure to add his notorious black storms to accentuate the double hung windows. The focal point of the home's exterior was a large wraparound porch with columns supporting a balcony. A Palladian-style window made from leaded glass perfectly crowned the projecting roof. With emphasis on main floor detail and design, large cherry wood doors with leaded-glass sidelights greeted guests at the front vestibule. Mosaic wood floors, pocket doors and intricately carved wood fretwork above the stairs were just a few of the majestic details. Dayton was a trustee of the Westminster Presbyterian Church and showcased the Dayton House by teaching Sunday school and hosting numerous church events at the home.

In 1902, the Daytons uprooted and moved to Minneapolis, Minnesota, where he founded Dayton's Dry Goods Store, which later became Dayton's department store. A man who believed in giving back to the community, he donated large sums of money to the Worthington church and established the Dayton Foundation. He even served on a committee called the Community Fund, which today is known as United Way. His sons would take over his business, and in 1962, the Daytons began the Target discount store.

But as Dayton went on to achieve great success, his original home in Worthington was slowly falling apart. The Worthington community demonstrated great leadership and pride in the grand home and fought to no end to save it from disrepair. Two other families would reside in the home before it would be turned into a nursing home/boardinghouse. Historic Worthington Inc., a local nonprofit group, purchased the property for $150,000 with plans to preserve the historic structure that needed much repair. The next year, the home was placed on the National Register of Historic Places and received a preservation award from the Minnesota Preservation Alliance. The cost of the two-year restoration totaled $2 million. Today, the restored house is used as a bed-and-breakfast and reception hall for social gatherings. It's considered one of the city's gems and is held in high regard by the Worthington community.

Highly respected and sought after by successful men like Dayton, one might consider Dow a leader during his time. Described as quiet in nature and often avoiding the press, Dow most likely preferred it that way. Rather than promoting himself, he promoted his buildings and the worldly designs he brought to the table. One of the best examples of Dow's ability to expose a small territory town to big eastern influences was his love of the Richardsonian Romanesque style of architecture. Although he was known for creating his own hybrid of designs and was quick to create plans to suit his client's desires and lifestyle, when given the chance, Dow returned to the Romanesque style frequently. In fact, it was this style that brought the most attention to his work and the city.

One man in particular whom Dow idolized for his style was Henry Hobson Richardson, an international architect who mastered the Romanesque style and even had his name associated with it. Romanesque design is characterized by round arches that resemble those of ancient Roman architecture. Richardson spent most of his brief twenty-one-year career perfecting building solutions that pushed the boundaries of Romanesque design and created formulas to adapt his personal style to a wide range of building types. Eventually known as Richardsonian Romanesque, many architects, such as Dow, used variations of his design for smalltown and large-scale libraries, campus buildings, train depots, courthouses, commercial blocks and even residential homes.

Chapter 5

THE GREAT DAKOTA BOOM

The first railroads ushered in what was called the Great Dakota Boom decade of the 1880s. The population of Sioux Falls swelled from over 2,100 in 1880 to over 10,000 at the end of the span. Ironically, the boom coincided with Dow's most prosperous decade, which was referred to as his golden years. As commissions came rolling in from the bustling industries, Sioux Falls citizens' newfound wealth funded some of his best creations. Between railroads, quarries and divorces, Sioux Falls began to grow at an exponential rate.

The first railroad entered Dakota Territory in 1872, but work stalled not long after due to poor economic conditions. Three years later, the need arose once again in Sioux Falls to secure a railroad. Community interest was there, but a good crop was needed before the Sioux Falls Railway Commission would be convinced. Finally, in 1877, an overflowing wheat crop provided the impetus to move forward with securing a railroad. By the next year, local papers announced grading had begun. Soon the rails had been laid and the cumbersome task of building bridges out of timber was conquered. Local residents anxiously awaited as the project slowly inched its way to Sioux Falls.

Numerous tracks were formed across Dakota Territory and the surrounding region, but it was the Great Northern Railway that completed one of the largest efforts in connecting Sioux Falls and Dakota Territory. The railroad entered Dakota Territory from the northeast and would reach numerous cities such as Aberdeen, Watertown, Huron, Sioux Falls

The expansion of railroads was a vital part in the 1880s population explosion known as the Great Dakota Boom. *Siouxland Heritage Museums.*

and Yankton. Soon after, another significant railroad made its way to Sioux Falls. The Illinois Central Railroad, a subsidiary of the Rock Island Railroad, connected Sioux Falls to Watertown and Minneapolis/St. Paul to Watertown.

Not only did railroads increase opportunity and ultimately bring the Dow brothers to Dakota Territory, but they also created a demand for the construction of depots. Later in his career, Dow would be commissioned to design a number of train stations that offered travelers a wondrous welcome of fine architecture as they entered the city. In 1886, Dow designed the Rock Island Depot, originally known as the Burlington, Cedar Rapids & Northern Railroad Depot, on East Tenth Street. Using a Richardsonian Romanesque–influenced design, managers of the new depot wanted to create something that reflected their newfound status. The exterior was built of Sioux Falls' celebrated jasper designed in a random ashlar pattern, but it was the interior that included a striking and unique feature. It was called Georgia pine, the only wood of this kind that had ever been used in the city at that time. It was utilized throughout the interior as a testament to the celebrated Burlington Road. As all the elements came together, the building was considered one of the finest small railroad depots in the country. By 1950, passenger service had ended, and only freight was hauled for the next twenty years before the railroad was abandoned in 1970. Today, the depot has been placed on the National Register of Historic Places and has been converted into a museum.

Railroads also made their way through smaller suburbs of Sioux Falls that capitalized on the new form of transportation during the Great Dakota Boom. The small town of Rowena was said to have experienced more growth than any other western town in the 1880s. Located east of Sioux Falls, it was cited that twenty elegant buildings existed in the town, one of them being the Illinois Central Depot. In 1887, the citizens of Rowena wanted an elegant building that surpassed the ordinary passenger depots located at other points, so they paid out of their own pockets to commission Dow to draw plans for a depot better suited to their tastes. Dow went on to construct an urban-style depot that featured a jerkinhead roofline. Theories exist that both this depot and a two-story wooden residential home designed by Dow were moved outside Rowena and are currently used as residential homes.

Quartzite was in high demand, and soon a famed quarry located outside Sioux Falls would dominate the paving-stone industry and create yet another suburb. It was called East Sioux Falls, the direct result of a vision from the quarry kingpin C.W. Hubbard. Owning the Sioux Falls Granite Company, Hubbard ruled the quarry industry in Sioux Falls. He soon expanded his vision, eyeing land and stone located east of Sioux Falls. It didn't take long before he would invest $150,000 and expand his quarry business to create a

The Illinois Central Depot was built in 1887 and also reflected the newfound status of an up-and-coming town. It's said that the townspeople paid out of their own pockets to commission Dow to create the elaborate depot. *Siouxland Heritage Museums.*

Above: The 1888 Barn, as it's called today, was built by Dow for the small Sioux Falls suburb called East Sioux Falls. Most of the town's buildings were simple and appropriate for a quarry town. This barn was a rare commission, as it featured some unique detailing. *Bill Hoskins.*

Opposite, top: One of the quarries located in East Sioux Falls. Most of the stone from these quarries was used by Dow to construct his elaborate buildings. *Siouxland Heritage Museums.*

Opposite, bottom: The occupation of stonecutting during the 1800s provided lucrative rewards; however, most of the men fell victim to the hazards later in life. *Siouxland Heritage Museums.*

township. But unlike its "big sister," East Sioux Falls was not about attracting settlers with grand structures and elaborate homes. Hubbard's vision was to build a town around a quarry. It was to be self-sustaining, with most of its population being stonecutters and their families. He saw very little need to construct bold buildings that gave the appearance of a prosperous town. East Sioux Falls had only one purpose, and that was to quarry stone. The East Sioux Falls quarry quickly became a leader, with its output used to construct many of Dow's designs, including his grand depots in Sioux Falls.

In 1888, Dow constructed a uniquely designed stable for the small town. It rivaled other plain buildings such as the simplistic worker cottages, boardinghouse, slaughterhouse, general store and school. Other than Dow's stable, the suburb's only pride was a two-story town hall bearing a tall steeple.

But even that was constructed to house quarrymen who rented rooms located on the second level. Reports to Sioux Falls of a bustling community in East Sioux Falls spread. A progress report at the time noted a population of four hundred people, three hundred of whom were quarry workers. The major demand for stone from the heart of the small town was used primarily for paving and was exported to Chicago by the Illinois Central Railroad. It's ironic that the stone from the East Sioux Falls quarry was used to erect the grand depots in Sioux Falls, yet its own depot was a plain, modest timber structure. Unimpressive, this represented the mentality of the town and its development for functionality only.

At its peak in the late 1880s, it's reported that as many as one in five workers was employed in quarry-related work. The growing popularity of quartzite as a distinctive architectural element created a frenzy for talented stonecutters. Recruited from as far away as England, these highly skilled cutters were the only people who knew how to cut stone to fulfill the architectural demands, and the lure of high wages attracted the men to the area. Most didn't realize the hazardous health conditions that would cost them their life. The chipping away at the stone created a glass-like dust called silica. The basic component of quartzite, the silica dust was inhaled into their lungs. Breathing in the dust day after day caused a progressive, disabling and often fatal lung disease called silicosis, or stonecutters' consumption. It took years for the men to realize the hazards, and most were faced with an unpleasant death at a very young age.

Chapter 6

THE BEAUTY OF EDUCATION

Just as merchants and promoters were busy developing profitable businesses, the mark of an up-and-coming city also included the need for the culture and refinement that was made possible by education. No longer considered a luxury by rural citizens, R.F. Pettigrew immediately tapped into this need and didn't hesitate to dedicate much of his acquired land for the establishment of schools. From religious denominations to public institutions, the Great Dakota Boom produced a number of schools to which Dow would contribute his architectural skills. One of Dow's most notable works started in 1884, when he and Bishop Hare began collaborating on a number of educational buildings. Their relationship would continue throughout the rest of Dow's working years and would produce grand structures that provided the perfect outlet for Dow's creativity.

Episcopal missions were prominent in Dakota Territory during the 1880s thanks to the efforts of Bishop Hare, who went on to construct numerous mission boarding schools for the Native American population. These schools were often built for practical use rather than making any form of architectural statement. Hare was credited with building more Episcopal churches than anyone else during that time. The first Dow/Hare project was a simple Episcopal church called the New Hope School, which was located on a high bluff overlooking the Missouri River in Springfield, Dakota Territory. The Missouri River would be a catalyst in the development and success of Springfield as Native Americans, fur traders and the Corps of Discovery all harnessed the form of transportation. Officially formed in

1870, Springfield bore another profitable natural resource, as it was located on an eighty-foot chalkstone bluff that extended for miles. By 1874, the town was growing; several businesses were in operation, and a small newspaper called the *Springfield Times* began publication. It would go down in history as the oldest weekly newspaper published in South Dakota.

Bishop Hare commissioned Dow to design a boarding school for Native American children in 1884. Dow made the plans for a simple Queen Anne–style structure and utilized the native chalkstone. Because the stone was soft, it was required to be stuccoed with clay or cement to prevent erosion and was scored to restore the appearance of masonry. Making use of his plans for the basic structure, the Episcopal Church would construct a series of identical chapels on the Sioux reservations. Not elaborate, they played a significant role in many communities. Dow would be invited back to Springfield years later, only this time he was hired by the people rather than by Bishop Hare.

The second Dow-designed Episcopal school was built the following year, in 1885. Located eight miles northeast of the Rosebud Reservation, the Saint Mary's School accommodated twenty-five boys and twenty-five girls. A simple wood design, it was essentially a replica of the New Hope School in Springfield. Unlike his previous commission, the Saint Mary's School resided on land appropriated for a reservation rather than a township. The Rosebud Reservation wasn't officially established until 1889 by the United States' partition of the Great Sioux Reservation. Life on the reservation was extremely difficult due to poverty and a lack of jobs and opportunities, and many families were forced to leave. Dow and Bishop Hare's collaboration for the simple Saint Mary's School would go on to provide education to Native American children for many years.

Years later, Dow designed his third and final Episcopal school in collaboration with Bishop Hare. The Saint Elizabeth boarding school was built on the Standing Rock Reservation in 1890. Although remaining simplistic in design, this school differed in that the chapel was located to the right of the school and was connected by a long, covered walkway. Fire would claim the school in 1910, and Dow would be invited back to construct another school. At this time, Dow was heavily into experimental construction using concrete blocks, and he built the second Saint Elizabeth's boarding school using his newly invented Perfection Block Machine.

The success of colleges and universities in area towns got the residents of Springfield thinking. It was quickly decided that the township wanted to place more emphasis on design for its proposed plan and looked to Dow to carry forth with its vision. In the 1890s, the citizens of Springfield gathered

Saint Mary's School located on the Rosebud Indian Reservation was the second Episcopal school Dow designed with Bishop Hare. The first was one of Dow's first commissions, the New Hope School. *Siouxland Heritage Museums.*

to raise funds for the construction and operational needs for a higher educational system. A donation of forty thousand acres of land breathed new life into the town's dream. Residents reached into their own pockets to donate private partnerships; meanwhile, Governor John. A. Burbank donated a tract of land. After years of rallying and private fundraising, Springfield was given the go-ahead to hire Dow to construct the Main Hall for the Springfield Normal School in 1895. The new building, although not too elaborate, was made of sturdy stone and doubled the space of the original building. Eventually, wings were added to the main building, with dormitories and other buildings soon after. Its name was even changed to the University of Dakota in Springfield, giving official accreditation to its efforts. But Springfield would forever fight for its right to be a place of higher learning. After years of successful graduates, the once-esteemed learning center was closed in 1984. The final class of twenty-six graduates received their diplomas while the rumblings of trucks could be heard in the distance, hauling away college records and equipment in preparation to convert the campus into a prison. Today, the site is known as the Mike Durfee State Prison, with male inmates replacing the once-thriving campus life.

Known for diversity in working with his clients, little is said about whether Dow ever complained about the complexity and artistic opportunity for his design. Thankfully, there were a number of significant educational commissions that did allow the young architect to experiment with grand scales and stylistic advances. One of the most noteworthy came from a meeting between R.F. Pettigrew and Bishop Hare. In 1884, the duo set out on horse and buggy to a site located on the west side of town. Under Pettigrew's lead, Bishop Hare was convinced that Sioux Falls would be a good site for a school. Bishop Hare was persuaded to construct an educational institute for young ladies of the missionaries serving in the western Dakota Territory. But Bishop Hare offered to build on one stipulation: the city had to come up with a site and $10,000 in cash. Each of these conditions was met, and work began to construct a main classroom for what would be named the All Saints School in Sioux Falls.

Dow went to work and chose to use myriad stones, with the main portion of the building Sioux quartzite trimmed with dark red pipestone. The first building housed the chapel, dining room, library, parlors, lounges, labs and classrooms. The main school was topped with a unique observatory, while the chapel heralded a bell tower. He also employed gables, towers, belvederes and contrasting scale in his design. A final embellishment was a set of stained-glass windows created by Mr. Tiffany himself for the chapel. Additional buildings were later added to the campus, each with intricate details. True examples of High Victorian Gothic architecture,

Dow chose to design the All Saints School in a High Victorian Gothic style. It is revered as one of the most dramatic Episcopal schools he would design with Bishop Hare. *Siouxland Heritage Museums.*

these structures remain as attractive landmarks in Sioux Falls and were the first Dow projects to be listed on the National Register of Historic Places. All Saints School is revered as one of the most dramatic of the many Episcopal schools and chapels Dow designed during his collaboration with "missionary Bishop" William Hare.

By the end of the Great Dakota Boom, four private institutions for higher education were in operation in Sioux Falls. Like All Saints School, Dow was given the opportunity to provide designs for many of them. One project that provided Dow with a blank canvas to create his unique hybrid of architectural styles was Meredith Hall. Named in honor of Reverend E.B. Meredith, the first president of the newly developed college called the Dakota Collegiate Institute, the building was constructed in 1883 and featured a mansard roof of the Second Empire style, a raised central pavilion and plain dormer windows. Over the next decade, the school would be renamed several times, and today it is known as the University of Sioux Falls. Sadly, the unique stone structure known as Meredith Hall was razed in the 1950s.

The need for education in Sioux Falls wasn't just important to businessmen like R.F. Pettigrew; even the general public had a vested interest in securing Sioux Falls as the location of choice for numerous universities. In 1889, when the Norwegian Evangelical Lutheran Synod proposed a Lutheran Normal Training School, citizens joined forces and raised $5,600 as seed money. Pettigrew and his business partner, S.L. Tate, followed suit and donated four acres of land. Dow was awarded the commission to build a fine stone structure at the cost of $25,000, with the remaining expenses to be paid by the Lutheran Synod. Later, the building was called Old Main when the campus became Augustana College.

Despite the lure of settlers to create a new society out of the prairie wilderness, the citizens saw a need for a school to serve a small number of deaf children in the territory. In 1880, two experienced teachers had been recruited to serve a handful of deaf children. They operated out of a boardinghouse until years later, when legislature appropriated $2,000 to develop a school on a 10.0-acre site of land in Sioux Falls. The project that locals had said was built of "human compassion" would later be built of stone. Dow was the perfect architect to carry forth the mission to erect four structures to create a school for the hearing impaired. Located on 23.5 acres of land, the State School for the Deaf would eventually consist of thirteen buildings.

But back in 1883, the campus began with the construction of the Deaf Mute Main Building, which was also referred to as Old Main. Later, the

The main building of All Saints School in Sioux Falls was an elaborate design that included the use of native Sioux quartzite and featured many embellishments. Today, it is fully restored and listed on the National Register of Historic Places. *Siouxland Heritage Museums.*

Meredith Hall was named after Reverend E.B. Meredith. Constructed in 1883, the Second Empire–style building included a mansard roof, raised central pavilion and dormer windows. *Siouxland Heritage Museums.*

The four original buildings on the State School of the Deaf in Sioux Falls were a community project that started with the construction of a main building (otherwise referred to as Old Main), dormitory, workshop and barn. The campus would later expand to a total of thirteen buildings. *Siouxland Heritage Museums.*

territorial legislature appropriated $12,000 to erect a dormitory, workshop and barn. The students learned painting, carpentry and farming with the goal of bringing the deaf into the world of the hearing through a self-sustaining campus. Three of the buildings were composed of quartzite with trimmings of dark and light and reflected the same Victorian Romanesque style as All Saints School but not nearly as elegantly appointed. Today, the South Dakota School for the Deaf, as it has been renamed, still remains, serving the community of Sioux Falls. Two of Dow's original quartzite structures act as iconic hubs for the vast campus.

A growing population meant a surge in student school enrollment. Although Dow did few public educational projects in Sioux Falls, his work in providing the city with beautiful places to learn made a mark during their time. Dow was commissioned to design the Longfellow School Building

Longfellow School in Sioux Falls was built in 1884. Dow chose a Queen Anne design rather than the traditional Italianate that was used in most public schools at the time. *Siouxland Heritage Museums.*

Lincoln School was one of the grandest public schools Dow would design in Sioux Falls. He chose the famous Richardsonian Romanesque style that included symmetry, semicircular windows and striking towers. *Siouxland Heritage Museums.*

(named after famed poet Henry Wadsworth Longfellow) in 1884 shortly after his move from Yankton. Serving as the fourth public school in Sioux Falls, it was located on Fourteenth Street and Seventh Avenue. Dow chose to veer away from the traditional Italianate schools by selecting a Queen Anne design with gable ends and several stone belt courses. Rather than stone, the building featured pressed brick with windows placed tall enough so students couldn't look out. The school remained in use until 1914 before being used as a warehouse and eventually razed.

Within a few years, Dow was in demand again by the school board. This time, the commission would be much grander and would utilize his love for Sioux quartzite. In honor of Abraham Lincoln, Dow's Lincoln High School was made up of six rooms and was located on Ninth Street and Grange Avenue. For the specified cost of $20,000, Dow used symmetry and semicircular window arches commonly found in the Richardsonian Romanesque style he often favored at the time. Although striking in appearance, the school would become a casualty of the wrecking ball; a mere twenty-five years later, it was razed to make way for a more modern school building.

Chapter 7

SHAPING DOWNTOWN

As Sioux Falls became more refined, it was clear that agriculture wasn't the main source of economy. Businesses sprung up along downtown streets, giving the community a host of shopping centers, restaurants and markets. To ensure Sioux Falls put forth its best effort to entice and retain local citizens and tourists, many business owners and merchants sought out only the best to attract their customers. At the time, the best was Wallace Dow.

It was common in the nineteenth century to utilize the Italianate style for commercial construction. This typically featured a shop front at the ground level, ordered windows above and a flat roofline with a parapet. But looking at Dow's compilation of commercial projects, it's evident that he didn't remain pure to one style alone but rather utilized myriad elements to create his own personal design. The few designs Dow provided for private businesses were on a much smaller scale than his governmental projects, but they swayed from the conventional Italianate and eventually showcased his love for the Richardsonian Romanesque.

One of Dow's finest examples of experimentation with Italianate style was the Metropolitan Block. Built for Harry Hollister in 1886 at a cost of $40,000, Dow used Victorian-era detailing and featured a unique corner entrance. Hollister, originally from the Chicago area, had a talent for banking, real estate investing and progressive business development. Dow delivered an equally progressive building. The first story was native Sioux quartzite, but Dow chose pressed brick for the top levels. It

The Union Trust Block located in downtown Sioux Falls was composed of rough-cut quartzite on the main level and pressed brick for the upper levels. Dow utilized a Queen Anne influence, which turned the creation into another Richardsonian Romanesque design. *Siouxland Heritage Museums.*

featured steam heating and electric lighting and housed the Minnehaha National Bank from 1886 to 1898. Later, the building was called the Dakota Block. Similar to the Metropolitan Block, Dow designed another corner entrance block in 1888 called the Union Trust Block. This Queen Anne–influenced design also housed a bank on the main level and was composed of rough-cut quartzite on the main level and pressed brick, which turned this creation into a Richardsonian Romanesque business block.

The rise of fraternal organizations led to Dow's next commission for the Masonic Building Association. It would come as no surprise that the Masons were leaders in designing grand halls with exotic styles. Although Dow was never a member of the fraternal organization, he did have a role in constructing a grand hall worthy of its use. With a striking resemblance to the Metropolitan Block, the city's first Masonic Temple was constructed in 1883 and was located at the southwest corner of Phillips Avenue and Tenth Street.

At a staggering cost of $100,000, the temple building housed retail shops on the ground floor and offices on the second, with the third dedicated to the lodge. Dow gave character to the Victorian-style building by employing three-dimensional wall and roof embellishments. A mansard roof and a tower gave the temple a Second Empire flavor. A large window on the third floor allowed sunlight to fill the lodge space. After the Minnehaha National Bank moved out of the Metropolitan Block in 1889, it found its new home in the similar stylings of the Masonic Temple. The bank would conduct business here until 1929. As for the Masons, they would utilize the third-floor lodge until 1905, when real estate developer and mason Porter Peck ordered a new temple building to be constructed due to the growth of the fraternal order. The original 1883 building, which was owned by the Masonic Building Association, was then sold to Peck.

Real estate and banking were quickly becoming the leaders in Phillips Avenue construction. As the businesses flourished, more banks and developers employed Dow to construct grand gestures of what was behind the continued growth of the city. William Van Eps, a well-known businessman, was one of the earliest pioneers of the city. A native of Minnesota, Van Eps came from humble beginnings. He traveled around the region, often employed in farm work and forced to carry all his earthly possessions on foot as he made his way to his next venture. In 1870, Van Eps heard word of a military reservation in Sioux Falls that was on the fringe of being abandoned. A true pioneer, he moved to Dakota Territory and took over the ground a year later. It was said that he became infatuated with the country and the realization that a city of considerable importance could be built on the plains of Dakota. During these early years, only a few officers and men endured the harsh lands.

The city's first Masonic Temple was constructed in 1883 and was located in downtown Sioux Falls. It housed a bank and offices, while the lodge operated out of the third floor. *Siouxland Heritage Museums.*

By 1886, Van Eps was an established businessman and could employ an architect like Dow to construct the Van Eps Block, located on Phillips Avenue. One of the several blocks built for his businesses, it was three stories high and demonstrated traditional Italianate design. It housed the Sioux Falls National Bank and other retail businesses on the ground

William Van Eps was an early pioneer who became infatuated with the Midwest region, mostly the area around the falls on the Big Sioux River. He set out on foot in 1870 with big dreams for a prosperous city. Van Eps remained living in Sioux Falls for decades and continued to promote the city. *Siouxland Heritage Museums.*

floor. The building, although it didn't demonstrate many artistic embellishments, must have impressed Dow. His business letterhead showed he utilized this building for his own architectural business.

Dow continued with more basic Italianate trends when designing a building for the local chapter of the national Civil War veteran group named the Joe Hooker Post No. 10, Grand Army Republic (GAR). Hooker had an impressive career as an officer in the United States Army. He achieved the rank of major general during the Civil War. It's noted that the Sioux Falls post was the single most powerful political investment group of nineteenth-century America.

The local chapter building, called the GAR Hall, was also referred to as the Briggs and Robinson Building, as they operated their real estate and insurance business from the second floor. The three-story building used a combination of pressed brick and polished stone trimmings and was lit by both gas and electricity. As was typical with downtown blocks, the ground level was dedicated to retail. Eventually, the GAR sold the building to Joseph Bailey Jr. after a library was built. Renamed once again, the structure became known as the Bailey-Glidden Block, and members of the GAR moved their meetings to the library basement. But the three letters etched in the parapet typically led most to call it the GAR Hall.

One of the finest examples of Romanesque Revival design was seen in Dow's iconic Peck, Norton and Murray Block, nestled in the heart of downtown Sioux Falls. Dow was originally employed to construct the three-story brick building for Porter Peck, a real estate developer. John F. Norton, the mayor of the city from 1887 to 1889, and John Murray, a farm implement dealer who was in business with Norton, later joined

BANK

G.A.R.
HALL

Above: The trio of Romanesque buildings known as the Peck-Norton-Murray Block located on Phillips Avenue in Sioux Falls housed both offices and storerooms and featured numerous architectural embellishments. *Siouxland Heritage Museums.*

Opposite, top: The Van Eps Block demonstrated traditional Italianate design with few artistic embellishments. This building is where Dow would operate his architectural business for many years. *Siouxland Heritage Museums.*

Opposite, bottom: The GAR Hall, also known as the Bailey-Glidden Block, was a combination of pressed brick and polished stone trimmings. The ground level was dedicated to retail and also housed the YMCA. *Siouxland Heritage Museums.*

Peck. The trio commissioned Dow to build an impressive line of buildings that would hold both offices and storerooms. The design, developed by Dow, was decorated with elements of several architectural styles but was more Romanesque than other commercial designs. Whether it was personal preference or Dow striving to convey urban progress, he was beginning to favor Romanesque design and began to utilize the motif in commercial commissions.

Porter Peck also commissioned Dow to construct the Peck & Campbell Livery located on Main Avenue. The Peck and Campbell Livery was owned by Porter Peck and Benjamin Franklin Campbell and was described as a magnificent structure two stories tall and featuring a mansard roof. It was later torn down to make way for the Mulhull Block.

Although the quartzite industry was in full swing, exporting tons of paving stones to surrounding cities by railroad, Dow, being an artist, didn't confine himself to using only native stone for his commissions. Even though the exportation of the product helped boost business for Sioux Falls, locals scoffed when Sioux Falls buildings featured alternative building materials such as pressed brick. To remedy this, Dow was quickly employed to construct a quartzite-clad skyline for downtown Sioux Falls.

The first all-quartzite building was the Temple Court, otherwise known as the Eddy-Davenport Block. This three-story, three-bay-wide building was the first of many impressive stone buildings.

The largest all-quartzite building was the impressive Edmison-Jamison Block. In fact, it was one of the largest stone masonry buildings in the area. Built in 1890 at a cost of $87,000, the simple six-story, rock-faced façade was boosted by detail and heavy Romanesque corner arches. This symbolic stone building also represented Dow's implementation of a style of architecture known as the Chicago School, an influence that Henry Hobson Richardson also favored.

Famous throughout the world, the Chicago School style is also known as the Commercial style. During the turn of the twentieth century, the Chicago School was a school of architects who were the first to promote new technologies of steel-frame construction in commercial buildings and dabbled in European Modernism. Distinguishing features of the Chicago School also include masonry cladding and large plate-glass windows with limited amount of exterior ornamentation. Dow chose to bring this style of big-city architecture to the young city.

The Edmison-Jamison Block stood proudly on the corner of the southwest corner of Ninth Street and Phillips Avenue and would later be known as the Minnehaha Block. Individual in nature, it was the tallest building in Sioux Falls until 1912 and contained seventy-one rooms, five storerooms and seven apartments. In 1947, new regulations forced the top stories to be removed. Dow's grand open staircase topped by a skylight and the fact that fire equipment couldn't reach the upper levels were major factors for the modification. Left with only four stories, the remainder of the once-grand structure was prone to the postwar

The Temple Court was the first all-quartzite-clad building in downtown Sioux Falls. Otherwise known as the Eddy-Davenport Block, the three-story building was the first of many quartzite creations. *Siouxland Heritage Museums.*

The Edmison-Jamison Block was the largest all-quartzite building at a towering six stories high and utilized a Richardsonian Romanesque design. *Siouxland Heritage Museums.*

"modernization" of its first-floor façade. Virtually unrecognizable, it was eventually razed in 1980.

Dow turned to the Chicago School style of architecture that same year when constructing the Blauvelt Block. Built for Silas Blauvelt, the nephew of early pioneer William Van Eps, the structure was commissioned around 1890 to house the growing wholesale grocery business for Jewett Brothers & Jewett. This building utilized a clear division of three sections: a shop on the main level, a central section with vertical piers and a projecting cornice. Certainly not as grand as the Edmison-Jamison Block, it remained noteworthy as one of Dow's experiments with the Chicago School style.

Less vertical in scope, the Waples Block, located on Phillips Avenue, did employ the use of native Sioux quartzite. Built in 1885 for Robert Coulter Waples, the building later would be known as the Van Brunt Building. Waples himself would also be known by another name: Commodore Waples. A true demonstration of how easily a title could be acquired, legend has it that while Mr. Waples was exiting a train in Iowa, he was mistakenly addressed as Commodore Vanderbilt due to his dapper looks. From that day on, he was always known as Commodore Waples.

Phillips Avenue was booming with business when attention turned to growing another downtown street. In 1884, E.A. Sherman began the development of Main Avenue. Sherman was an early pioneer who was engaged in a number of different ventures. He was half owner of the *Sioux Falls Independent* newspaper for a while and was even superintendent of the Minnehaha County schools. Later, he was elected to the Republican state legislature and was president of numerous banks. He believed in the future of Sioux Falls and wanted to construct a street that would expand business development from Phillips Avenue.

One of Sherman's first projects in 1885 was the Cascade Block, located on Main Street between Ninth and Tenth Streets. The two-story pressed brick building was sixty-six feet by ninety feet with four spaces on the first floor and eight suites and offices on the second. The front façade was built of cut stone, iron, French plate glass and St. Louis pressed brick. At the time, St. Louis bricks were in high demand. The clay found in the St. Louis area was said to be the finest in the country, and nearly 100,000 tons of bricks were shipped out every year, making St. Louis one of the largest brick-manufacturing cities in the world. The Cascade Block was built for eastern capitalists, and Dow's brother Wilbur received the steam and plumbing contract for the building.

The Sherman Block was a three-story brick building that housed early county offices before the new courthouse was built in 1890. *Siouxland Heritage Museums.*

But it was the commission for the building named after Sherman himself that was a true honor for Dow. This building, although not unique in design, was vital to the development of Sioux Falls. The Sherman Block was a three-story brick building that housed the early county offices before the new courthouse was built in 1890 and served as the post office before the Federal Building was constructed in 1895. Just as Sherman himself was boundless in his talents, his building proved to be diverse in its use. In 1898, the Sherman Block was remodeled and converted into the New Theatre, which took a vivid turn from its staunch business background and looked more toward entertaining the public.

Although the Sherman Block was razed in 1916, Sherman and his buildings still take credit for expanding the business district that had once been confined to Phillips Avenue. Sherman would later partner with Mary C. Richardson to build the Sherman-Richardson Block on Ninth Street and Main Avenue. Both the Norberg Bros., veteran painters and decorators, and Chris Anderson, veteran shoemaker, would occupy the building before it was razed in 1937. Aside from building Main Street, Sherman would leave another legacy for the city of Sioux Falls. Following a prosperous career in business, his final occupation was law. He turned his interests into negotiating numerous land deals for the creation of city parks. Today, Sherman is still known as the "father of the park system."

Other Main Avenue commissions quickly rolled in for Dow. In 1890, he was at the peak of his career, and his work reflected his success. The Syndicate Block featured a six-bay Romanesque façade with a unique cast-iron and plate-glass first floor. He also utilized prefabricated parts to divide the larger windows on the upper floors. Intricate triptychs of smaller windows topped each arched window bay, demonstrating Dow's blend of the Romanesque design. Although composed of pressed brick, it was finished with stone trimmings. The four-story-high building was constructed at a cost of $60,000 and contained many forward-thinking interior features such as an elevator and fifty-eight furnished living rooms. The main floor housed retail and the Citizens Bank. Named the Syndicate Block because it was utilized as a syndicate, numerous successful businessmen touted the structure

During the peak of Dow's career, he designed the Syndicate Block in 1890. The six-bay Romanesque façade featured a cast-iron and plate-glass first floor. *Siouxland Heritage Museums.*

Dow designed the City Auditorium in a mere six months with the intent to hold the 1899 convention of the National Butter Maker's Association. *Siouxland Heritage Museums.*

as a way to promote the northern part of Sioux Falls as a business district. Later, the building was purchased by Joseph Kirby and became known as the Western Surety Building before being razed in 1962 to make room for the First Bank of South Dakota.

In 1898, Dow was called upon for quite an unusual commission or, rather, an unusual catalyst for construction. The Sioux Falls Business Men's League went above and beyond typical efforts to lure the National Butter Maker's Association to hold its 1899 convention in the city of Sioux Falls. Obviously, the thought of these butter makers holding their convention in Sioux Falls must have had quite an impression to erect a building with the intentions to hold their gathering. Nonetheless, Dow went on to build what was called the City Auditorium at Ninth Street and Dakota Avenue. Unlike his massive Romanesque quartzite creations, the auditorium was unique in design but took on a more simplistic style with arched doorways and corner turrets. Whether it was the changing fashion of architecture or the result of expedited orders, the Sioux Falls Business Men's League moved quickly to build a facility large enough to house the convention. Dow was given a mere six months to design and execute the plan.

Aside from the convention, the building would also serve as a combination auditorium and city hall. Although the exterior was not stuccoed and city offices were not complete, the auditorium was ready and waiting for the butter makers by the end of January 1899. Deemed a success, it went on to be used as the city's fire station. A large timber fire tower, originally built in 1884 at Ninth Street and Dakota Avenue, was moved to the site in 1899. It housed the original fire bell that had alerted local volunteer firemen for decades. In 1912, a more sophisticated fire station was needed after countless fires claimed numerous buildings. The tower was moved to the new grand quartzite Central Fire Station at Ninth Street and Minnesota Avenue, and the original bell was incorporated into a larger stone tower. But after being struck by lightning in its new location, even that tower was shaved down. The original bell that had served the public since 1884 was retired and now proudly sits in front of what is today called Fire Station #1. As for the Sioux Falls City Auditorium, it was razed in 1934 to make room for the current city hall.

Chapter 8

THE CROWN AND ITS JEWELS

South Dakota had just achieved statehood in 1889 when the thriving city of Sioux Falls put demands on the government for larger, more substantial public institutions. The allotted space for the county courthouse in the Sherman Block was tight and in need of expansion. The timing was just right for Dow. In the height of his golden years, he had already shaped the landscape of downtown and was about to put the crown jewel in the area when he was awarded the commission for the Minnehaha County Courthouse. Although Dow had credibility, he received the project by one vote of the county commissioners over a younger competitor, Joseph Schwartz. Dow apparently received the job because of the detailed nature of his bid and his willingness to get bonded to guarantee that the building's cost would not exceed $80,000.

Joseph Schwartz began practicing architecture in 1887 and was one of Dow's first notable rivals. Schwartz moved with his family to Dakota Territory during the 1880s. Trained as a cabinetmaker and working for a contracting company, he established his career in Sioux Falls and many other eastern South Dakota communities. Although his focus was mainly on church commissions for Catholic parishes, he did bid on numerous projects alongside Wallace Dow, one being the famed Minnehaha County Courthouse. Schwartz lost the commission mainly due to his bid of $100,000, which was deemed too high for the county commissioners. Ironically, Dow's lower bid of $80,000 would escalate; the grand total for the building would be $100,000. Despite this rivalry, Dow had already

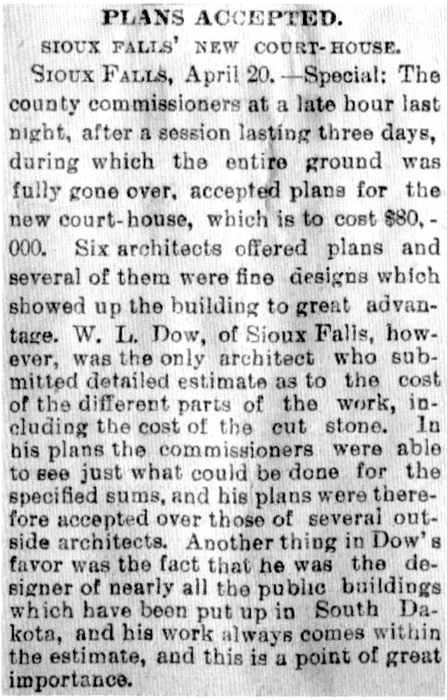

PLANS ACCEPTED.

SIOUX FALLS' NEW COURT-HOUSE.

Sioux Falls, April 20.—Special: The county commissioners at a late hour last night, after a session lasting three days, during which the entire ground was fully gone over, accepted plans for the new court-house, which is to cost $80,000. Six architects offered plans and several of them were fine designs which showed up the building to great advantage. W. L. Dow, of Sioux Falls, however, was the only architect who submitted detailed estimate as to the cost of the different parts of the work, including the cost of the cut stone. In his plans the commissioners were able to see just what could be done for the specified sums, and his plans were therefore accepted over those of several outside architects. Another thing in Dow's favor was the fact that he was the designer of nearly all the public buildings which have been put up in South Dakota, and his work always comes within the estimate, and this is a point of great importance.

A local newspaper article touting the construction and selection of W.L. Dow to build the Minnehaha Courthouse. The article included a number of Dow's other contributions to the city. *Siouxland Heritage Museums.*

established himself as the "prairie architect" and was often chosen because of his credibility and his large number of highly successful commissions throughout the territory.

Newspapers praised the decision to elect Dow as architect, and construction began in 1889 with workmen quarrying on the very site on which the building would stand. Some of the stone was used for the foundation; meanwhile, the basement would literally rest on the living bedrock. The building would be the best of the best, constructed solely of Sioux quartzite. The Richardsonian Romanesque design would be exquisite in detail and powerful in scale, with a 165-foot clock tower, making it the tallest structure between Chicago and Denver at that time. But at one point, the county commission grew concerned about the escalating costs and made the decision to omit the striking feature. Dow objected to this cost-saving strategy and went on to write up a petition that was signed by seventy-eight prominent residents to demand that the tower be kept in the plan. The county commission relented, and the symbolic tower continued its journey to the clouds.

Dow was clearly making a statement, and the Sioux Falls community was right alongside, claiming its permanence to the state through such an elaborate building. Guests are first greeted by perfectly symmetrical stone globes located at the base of the entrance steps; meanwhile, the elegant sloping roof angles and the rugged, massive appearance of its arched doors and windows are outward symbols of a city that's going places. Completed in 1890, the building would be known as one of Dow's greatest contributions to Sioux Falls architecture and would show visitors the capabilities of using native stone.

An early sketch of the Minnehaha Courthouse. It's noted that from the beginning, Dow's plans included the 165-foot clock tower. *Siouxland Heritage Museums.*

And the amenities were just as worthy as its beauty. Wallace Dow employed his brother, Wilbur, to design the sophisticated plumbing and heating, adding to the list of interesting features the Dow brothers contributed. Indoor flush toilets, a state-of-the-art ventilation system, electric lights and steam heat were just a few of the structural elements this building would be known for.

Completed in 1890, Dow's greatest contribution was the Minnehaha County Courthouse. The grand building provided a massive appearance for the purpose of luring potential citizens and businesses. *Siouxland Heritage Museums.*

Investors quickly took note of what was to take place surrounding such a gem. Upon completion of the Minnehaha County Courthouse and the construction of the Sixth Street Bridge crossing the Big Sioux River, a building boom suddenly spurred what was to be known as the "Courthouse District." Businessmen scrambled to erect equally grand blocks and did so with confidence. The famed courthouse designer was sought after to further ignite the competition among the business owners. Such friendly rivalry between six leading citizens led to a bet that their building blocks must be completed by November 1, 1890. It was taken so seriously that a binding agreement was drawn up that included a $1,000 fine if they did not comply with the contract.

One businessman who threw his hat in the race was Joel W. Parker. Parker was described as an endearing man and spirited citizen who worked with his son in the lumber business. He quickly hired the esteemed Dow to build a four-story building at a cost of $15,000. However, bids came in so high that Parker ended up with a three-story building at a cost of $20,000. Nonetheless, the Parker Block was majestic in appearance and a perfect gem to surround the main crown jewel. It was the original home of the Sioux Falls Candy Company, which was located on the main floor, and offices and apartments occupied the upper levels. By 1907, the building had been converted into a hotel, serving Sioux Falls during the days as the divorce capital and soldiers returning from war. Eventually falling into disrepair, new life was given to one of the original Courthouse District's gems through a massive restoration project. Today, it proudly serves the community and remains a beautiful companion to the courthouse.

Surrounding blocks, such as the Parker Block, were designed to be companions to Dow's famous Minnehaha County Courthouse. The Parker Block housed the Sioux Falls Candy Company before being converted into a hotel. *Siouxland Heritage Museums.*

Warner E. Willey and son-in-law Roy Williams also hired Dow to construct the Willey-Williams Block, located on Main Avenue. Dow designed an equally unique three-story structure to the Parker Block. However, Dow chose to use a dark orange-red pressed brick that created a blazing glow. With serpentine curves on the second and third stories, large bay windows were adorned with elaborate brickwork, stone windowsills and intricate detailing. Dow's Victorian Gothic design was another gem in the downtown crown, giving credit to businessmen Willey and Williams, who ran the Merchant Hotel located directly to the east. The two owners planned to use the upper level of the Willey-Williams Block as overflow hotel space for the Merchant Hotel, while the first floor was used for retail. In 1985, the building was restored, and it is still in use today.

Andrew C. Phillips was also looking to construct a grand building for his law practice and employed Dow to construct what was named the Law Exchange Block. Unlike the Parker Block and Willey-Williams Block, this building would be constructed out of an assortment of materials, including quartzite, pressed-brick walls, sandstone windowsills and polished granite pillars. A true Classic Revival gem, Dow took cues from the Chicago School style with a partial cast-iron façade and decorative brick cornices and window panels that added a twist Dow often used as his personal trademark style. In 1893, the landmark structure was renamed the Phillips Block in honor of its builder. The building would go on to house a number of businesses and take on several names. Today, it remains known as the Law Exchange Block and has been fully restored and is in use.

Opposite, top: The Willey-Williams Block provided a unique contrasting companion to the courthouse. For this commission, Dow selected bright pressed brick and intricate Victorian Gothic details like the serpentine curves and bay windows. *Brad Dumke.*

Opposite, bottom: Built for A.C. Phillips, the Law Exchange Block utilized an assortment of materials, including quartzite, pressed brick, sandstone and polished granite. *Siouxland Heritage Museums.*

Chapter 9

THE CITY OF HOMES

Businesses were booming, quarries were churning out stone and railroads had made Sioux Falls accessible for hundreds of tourists and potential citizens. It was time to refine a housing district. Wealthy businessmen, who may have already commissioned Dow to design their business blocks, needed places to hang their hats and saw potential in their personal residences as examples of pride and success. Dow was about to make his mark on what was referred to as Nob Hill, which coined the Sioux Falls term "City of Homes."

Other prominent cities, such as San Francisco, already boasted luxurious Nob Hills. The word "nob," being defined as a citizen with great wealth and success, was a fitting description for many Sioux Falls residents. Soon Nob Hill would find its home in the growing city of Sioux Falls and provided the perfect palette for Dow's creations. One of his first residential commissions on Nob Hill would be one of his most famous: the Avery House.

Henry M. Avery was owner of the Sioux Falls Abstract and Title Insurance Company. An active member of the Sioux Falls Fire Department, Avery was known as one of Sioux Falls' most energetic citizens and a true supporter of any project that would promote the prosperity of the city. His home certainly reflected such. One of the few Richardsonian Romanesque residential homes Dow would build, the project required so much quartzite that Dow needed to collaborate with C.W. Hubbard. A fine example of Romanesque reflections, the home boasts a round tower,

The iconic Avery House, built for Henry M. Avery, is one of Dow's purest Romanesque residential designs. Built of native quartzite, it features a round tower, slate roof and deeply recessed windows. *Siouxland Heritage Museums.*

slate roof, hipped and eyebrow dormers, belt courses and deeply recessed window openings. The interior was just as exquisite, with woodwork of oak, fir, birch, mahogany, maple and pine.

Part of a trio of quartzite Romanesque homes in Sioux Falls, the Avery House proudly stood on Prairie Avenue, where Nob Hill began taking shape. Avery's business partner, Frank Hyde, also contributed to the prestige of Nob Hill by enlisting in Dow's designs for his personal residence located on South Duluth Avenue.

In 1887, Dow's brother Wilbur commissioned him to design a more modest Richardsonian Romanesque home for his family. Located on Duluth Avenue, the home featured rock-faced quartzite walls and round-headed windows, which were typical of the style. Later, the home would be razed, but the legacy lives on. In the 1950s, a former Sioux Falls resident, Edmond N. Dolphay, of Detroit Lakes, Michigan, purchased the W.A. Dow home and began to dismantle the structure stone by stone to use the cut quartzite as building materials. At the time, it was called a "labor of love," as Dolphay painstakingly hauled each stone by hand to Detroit Lakes, where he reassembled the pieces into a four-bedroom lakeshore house. Portions of the original Dow home were also used for two other houses. It was said that during the dismantling, Dolphay discovered numerous interesting artifacts such as an 1889 Indian-head penny from Ed Dow, Girl Scout magazines dating shortly after the founding of the organization and *Argus Leader* newspapers from before the turn of the century. As a testament to the quality of Dow's workmanship, the walls of Wilbur Dow's home were constructed of quartzite that ranged in width from eighteen inches to three feet thick. Although the reassembled stone no longer resembled Dow's original work, remnants of the original can still be found. Dolphay rebuilt three stone fireplaces from the original home that were used in his residence and two other homes.

Joseph Bailey Jr. took note of Dow's quartzite-clad homes and commissioned him in 1888 to design the city's final pure Richardsonian Romanesque residential home. Bailey gained his wealth as a lawyer, banker and prominent Republican. The home featured classic Queen Anne stylistic elements that included a rock-faced front gable wall adorned with the popular checker work of the period. Later, other prominent citizens took over the ownership of the home, including Joseph Kirby, an entrepreneur who created a number of successful businesses. A lawyer, he ran his own practice, helped found the South Dakota Central Railway and was a longtime director of the Minnehaha National Bank (now known as the First National Bank in Sioux Falls). His most successful accomplishment was the establishment of the Western Surety Company. Later, Kirby would be inducted into the South Dakota Hall of Fame in 1933. Meanwhile, his home would be fully restored and placed on the National Register of Historic Places.

Aside from Richardsonian Romanesque design, Dow's body of residential work shows an emphasis on the popular Queen Anne design. Made popular during the 1880s, this style replaced the French-derived Second Empire as the "style of the moment." Originally formulated in

An early sketch of W.A. Dow's home. A brother to Wallace, his home was a more modest example of Romanesque residential designs. *Siouxland Heritage Museums.*

The W.A. Dow home was constructed in 1887 and featured an abundance of native Sioux quartzite. The home was later dismantled, and the quartzite was used to construct various other projects. *Siouxland Heritage Museums.*

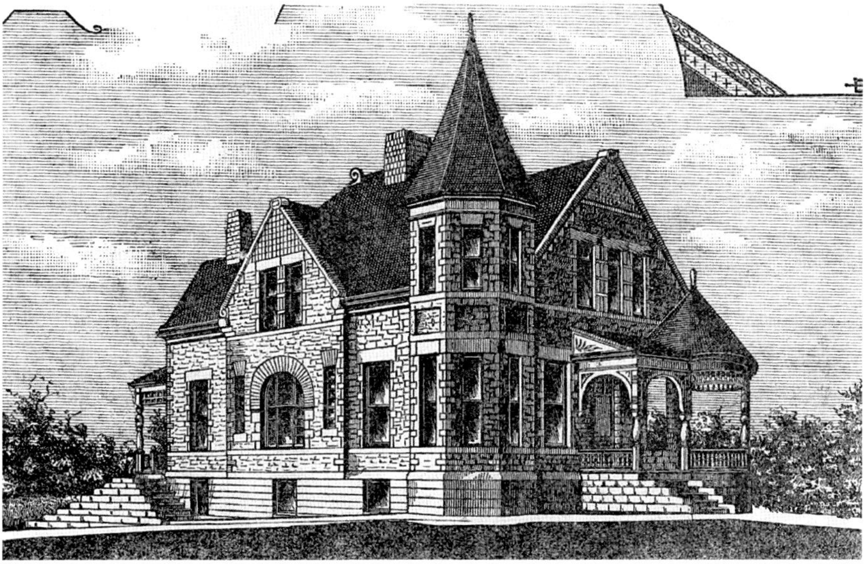

This early sketch of the Bailey-Edgerton-Kirby House showcased Dow's purest Richardsonian Romanesque residential homes in the city of Sioux Falls. *Siouxland Heritage Museums.*

The Kirby House, as it is called today, was built in 1888 of native Sioux quartzite. The more elaborate home features many embellishments such as deeply recessed windows and a large round tower. *Siouxland Heritage Museums.*

Britain, the style soon arrived at the New York House and School of Industry. From there, it took off, and Dow was one of the first to introduce the elegance to Sioux Falls. Elements of the American Queen Anne style included an asymmetrical façade, dominant front-facing gables, strong towers, wraparound porches, varying wall textures such as patterned wood shingles shaped into varying designs, dentils, columns, bay windows, monumental chimneys and leaded windows.

One of Dow's finest examples of Queen Anne elegance was the Charles C. Carpenter House, located on Duluth Avenue. Dow was summoned by one of Sioux Falls' earliest pioneers, Artemus Gale, to create a truly grand and unique home for his brother-in-law and sister, Charles and Frances Carpenter. Carpenter worked for the Dakota National Bank and was treasurer of the Sioux Falls Stockyards Company. His wife, Frances, was credited with building the famed Carpenter Hotel located downtown on Phillips Avenue. For their personal residence, Dow utilized outstanding features such as a first story of pressed brick with quartzite trimmings, while the upper portion was clad in slate fish-scale siding finished off with intricate spindle work.

The Carpenter House was one of Dow's most elegant Queen Anne homes in Sioux Falls. Located on Duluth Avenue, its many outstanding features include a first story of pressed brick with quartzite trimming. The upper portion used fish-scale slate and intricate spindle work. *Siouxland Heritage Museums.*

A companion to the Carpenter House, the Walts House was another creation of Queen Anne architecture. Located on Summit Avenue, the overly embellished home was completed in 1890 for Cyrus and Mary Walts. Dow remained true to form by including a tower, wraparound porch and multiplaned roof. Just as his home featured a variety of elements, Walts also held a variety of jobs in the up-and-coming city as the deputy postmaster, county superintendent of schools, clerk of the district court, county surveyor and city justice. His wife, Mary, was even the first public schoolteacher in Sioux Falls. The couple left a legacy both in work and in architecture. Together, they platted land in Sioux Falls and went on to have a city street named after them.

But when it came to exuberance, no home in Sioux Falls could top the elaborate Queen Anne scheme of the McMartin Residence. Thomas McMartin, an Iowa native, came to Sioux Falls in 1880 and began a long and successful career practicing law. He married Jennie Bowen in 1888 and soon began construction of their first home together. Her lavish taste and his wealth from "quickie" divorces gave Dow a residential design opportunity of a lifetime.

For the interior, the lush details included wall coverings of silk, imitation leather and embossed papers, while the polished tile fireplaces and stained-glass windows were classic elements for the Victorians. The McMartin Residence was a true display of Sioux Falls homeowners decorating their homes in the latest and most opulent tastes. Dow himself viewed this commission as an opportunity to display his talents while exposing other residents to urban design.

The McMartins lived in the home until 1911, when R.F. Pettigrew purchased it for $12,000. His intentions were to preserve the history of Sioux Falls and the surrounding regions through his personal collections. A world traveler and amateur archaeologist, his possessions grew so large that he built his own private museum on the rear of his home. In 1925, he opened his museum to the public. It was called the Pettigrew Home and Museum. It featured artifacts such as stone tools, Native American clothing, guns, natural history specimens and items collected during the early settlement of Dakota Territory. However, Pettigrew would see his museum open for only one year. In 1926, he passed away but willed his home and museum to the City of Sioux Falls with the stipulation that it be maintained as a museum. In the 1930s, the city built a further addition to the museum, fulfilling Pettigrew's intentions. Today, both the home and museum have been meticulously restored and are open to the public.

Built for the McMartin family, this grand Queen Anne home was such a fine example of elegance that R.F. Pettigrew later purchased it and built an addition to house a museum. The Pettigrew House and Museum are still in use today. *Siouxland Heritage Museums.*

The John Tuthill Residence was Dow showing his ability to reflect powerful urban character. Much like the McMartin-Pettigrew home, Dow was instructed to design a house that reflected Tuthill's status in the lumber business as the owner of a chain of thirty-two lumberyards. Dow quickly went to work designing an interior that exhibited an abundance of exotic woods such as Honduras mahogany, oak, maple, cherry, birch and redwood.

For the exterior, Dow included Romanesque detailing for the quartzite first floor, while the second and third took on a classic Queen Anne design with pyramidal and bell-shaped turrets that peered over the business district below. The wraparound porch included Ionic columns and dentil cornices, while the main block of the home intricately included floral garlands and Greek key patterns. Today, the turrets have been removed, but the home has been fully restored and serves as the bishop's residence for the Catholic Diocese of Sioux Falls.

An early sketch of the Tuthill House in Sioux Falls. The design included Romanesque detailing such as pyramidal and bell-shaped turrets and a large wraparound front porch. The interior featured a number of exotic woods to reflect Tuthill's occupation in the lumber business. *Siouxland Heritage Museums.*

A carpenter by trade, John M. Randolph commissioned Dow in 1902 to build a two-story Queen Anne residence on North Duluth Avenue. Unlike many of Dow's commissions, the Randolph family would own the home until 1972. The home, built of timber, featured a classic wraparound porch and a gable with turret and utilized multiple designs for the exterior. Today, the Randolph House has been fully restored and has been placed on the National Register of Historic Places.

Dow was becoming a master at designing homes that reflected the owner's status and occupation. Yet for Charles E. Johnson, Dow's choice of timber for his grand Queen Anne home was quite unusual. Johnson was a banker and investor in the Sioux Falls Granite Company. Although both Johnson and Dow had a penchant for native quartzite, the Johnson House was a unique Queen Anne hybrid design, despite the fact that no stone was used in the construction. Originally, patterned shingle siding and a projecting front gable typified Queen Anne design. However, to adapt to the changing architectural fashions, a wraparound porch with columns, a dentil cornice line, an elliptical fanlight and sidelights around

John Tuthill owned a chain of lumberyards and commissioned Dow to design an elaborate Queen Anne–style home that directly reflected his status in the lumber business. *Siouxland Heritage Museums.*

the front door were later added. In the early 1900s, Andrew Kuehn, a prominent wholesale grocer, purchased the home, and it became known as the Andrew Kuehn House.

In 1887, Charles E. McKinney commissioned Dow to build a home for him, his widowed mother and his half brother Judson Allen. Together, the brothers started the finance and investment firm of McKinney and Allen. An early settler of Sioux Falls, McKinney arrived in 1880 and, within two years, demonstrated his enterprising spirit by establishing the Sioux Falls National Bank, one of the earliest financial institutions. McKinney was made president, a position he would retain throughout the rest of his life. With his business located in the Dow-designed Van Eps Block, McKinney may have had exposure to his work. True to form, Dow designed a simple Queen Anne cottage that reflected McKinney's reputation for being enterprising yet cool-headed.

By 1903, architectural styles had changed significantly. Dow, being an esteemed architect, was open to new trends and didn't hesitate to experiment. In 1899, Paul F. and Mary L. Sherman began purchasing land on Nob

The Randolph House was built for John M. Randolph in 1902. The two-story Queen Anne home would remain in the Randolph family until 1972. It features a classic wraparound porch and gable with turret. *Siouxland Heritage Museums.*

Hill for their residence. With a desire to have a large lot, they purchased nearly three lots for their grand home. The Shermans selected Dow as their architect, and work began in 1902. The Shermans were heavily involved in the community. Paul was the president of the Minnehaha National Bank and was instrumental in developing the South Dakota Central Railroad to Watertown. Their home reflected a Greek Revival style, which took cues from the ancient Greek temple architecture. Quite unlike any other homes that Dow designed, utilizing this style for residential purposes allowed Dow to create a masterpiece with a large front porch with classic columns and

Sketch of the Johnson House in 1887. Charles E. Johnson was a banker and investor in the Sioux Falls Granite Company. Although both Johnson and Dow were vested in using quartzite, his residence was built of timber. *Siouxland Heritage Museums.*

The Johnson House featured a hybrid of Queen Anne style with its large wraparound porch, columns and dentil cornice line. In the early 1900s, Andrew Kuehn purchased the home, and it became known as the Johnson/Kuehn House. *Siouxland Heritage Museums.*

symmetrical façades. Quite like the Pettigrew Home and Museum, the Sherman Home was sold to the Knights of Columbus Hall in 1941 and was quickly repurposed for community use. Additional funding converted the garage into a Boy Scout building, and a large reception hall was later added to the west side of the house. Over the course of the next fifty years, work was done to maintain and update the home to serve the community as the Knights of Columbus Hall had done. Even surrounding homes were purchased for the purpose of additional parking. Located on Summit Avenue, this home still stands as a true testament to Dow's architectural capabilities and represents a community willing to put in the efforts to utilize a historic home for public use.

Homeowners often chose Dow after he had demonstrated his talents on their commercial blocks. This holds true for Joel W. Parker, whose home on North Minnesota Avenue was a partner to his business block on Main Avenue.

Although not as prestigious, homes were also being built in the southern parts of Sioux Falls, deemed Prospect Hill. A prominent Sioux Falls businessman, W.R. Kingsbury, commissioned Dow in 1884 to build

This early sketch of the Parker House shows Dow's love of elaborate detailing. The home was built for Joel W. Parker, the same businessman who enlisted Dow's talents for the Parker Block located in the Courthouse District. *Siouxland Heritage Museums.*

a Queen Anne home. At the time of completion, the home was quoted as having been "designed with particular reference to convenience, and just enough luxury and architectural ornamentation to satisfy the best taste." The home reflected an image of increasing urban influences and culture for Sioux Falls. Although simple in exterior ornamentation for a typical Queen Anne home, it took on a more sophisticated and cosmopolitan layout for its use. Being one of the first homes to include a conservatory, it reflected homes built in Chicago and the Twin Cities at the time. The unique circular greenhouse, or hothouse, boasted a conical roof just off the main portion of the home.

For Kingsbury, it was a reflection of his optimism. Kingsbury came to Sioux Falls in 1878 and worked in real estate until 1883. He was superintendent of the gasworks and later became president of the famed Dakota Rapid Transit and Railroad Company, which was the first motor line from Sioux Falls to East Sioux Falls.

Although the story of the Dakota Rapid Transit and Railroad Company was ill fated, it remains one of Sioux Falls' most aggressive acts to promote a city and a suburb. In 1889, a group of pioneering promoters came together and quickly formed the concept of a unique electric motor line to connect the "Queen City" of Sioux Falls to East

Built in the southern part of town known as Prospect Hill, the W.R. Kingsbury House featured urban influences and simple exterior ornamentation. It was the first home to include a conservatory, which Dow utilized as a design opportunity by creating a circular room with conical roof. *Siouxland Heritage Museums.*

Sioux Falls. It was not only the first of its kind, but it was also said to be the longest in the world. In the beginning, the line was initially intended to allow stonecutters to live in Sioux Falls rather than East Sioux Falls by providing easy and quick transportation. The line not only ran fast but also quite frequently throughout the day. Sioux Falls residents caught wind of the new venture and watched as the tracks were laid. It spanned six miles and required the construction of seven bridges. By 1890, it was complete, and Sioux Falls celebrated the historic occasion and boasted that the quarrymen would finally live in Sioux Falls. However, not all were happy with the venture. One such objector was R.F. Pettigrew. As the tracks were laid moving from east to west, it wasn't until they reached the western limits at Tenth Street and Phillips Avenue that a dispute broke out between the Dakota Rapid Transit and Railroad Company and Pettigrew and Tate's streetcar line. In the end, the tracks were laid for the Dakota Rapid Transit and Railroad Company, but Pettigrew and Tate immediately laid their own tracks to make certain there were no future advances.

A celebration of technology spread throughout the country, yet the electric motor line faced many obstacles. What had been intended as a "worker" line had expanded into recreational use, as Sioux Falls citizens enjoyed taking the leisurely ride to East Sioux Falls for picnics and sightseeing. But the economic crash of 1892, along with fierce winters and accidents, put a halt on the line. Soon, the transit faced financial constraints, which ultimately led to its demise in 1898. Over the years, the tracks have been removed, but the built-up bed on which the line ran could still be seen along the creek east of Sioux Falls for many years. Somewhat similar to the fate of the motor line, the Kingsbury Home was eventually hacked into small apartments, with the conservatory removed and the exterior stuccoed. Unlike the motor line, the structure remains in use today.

While Prospect Hill would never hold the same esteem as Nob Hill, the Robert Buchanan Residence on Summit Avenue may have been an attempt at acquiring the same status. Originally from Scotland, Robert Buchanan immigrated to Canada in 1842. In 1876, he came to Sioux Falls, where he started the *Sioux Falls Pantagraph*. He would later run a newspaper in Sioux Falls called the *Leader*, which eventually consolidated with the *Argus* in 1888 and was called the *Argus Leader*. Wallace's son, Baron Dow, would eventually run the newspaper. Buchanan's home no longer stands, but the *Argus Leader* remains as the city's top newspaper today.

The Sioux Falls Rapid Transit and Railway Company began in 1889 with the purpose to link Sioux Falls to East Sioux Falls. The electric motor line was the first of its kind and, at the time, the longest. *Siouxland Heritage Museums.*

Nobody could argue that when it came to Dow paying the bill for his own home, his understated and purpose-driven nature was the inspiration. He avoided Nob Hill but rather selected a less prestigious location in what was called Gale's Grove on First Avenue to build the W.L. Dow House. Irregular massing and an animated roofline reflect Queen Anne origins, and the home rests on a unique uncoursed quartzite foundation. Built in 1885, the main façade is composed of a series of gable ends that are adorned with brackets and floral motifs. A main gable allowed for a small balcony, while the side façades have projecting bays and small turret pipestone steps. Dow would live here with his family for fifteen years before he began to construct a forward-thinking dwelling on the same lot.

By this time, Edwin Dow had joined his father in the architectural trade. The new name W.L. Dow & Son soon became a mainstay in local newspapers. Proving once again that Dow personally preferred function over form, he went on to design a first-of-a-kind dwelling to house his family and his son Edward's. Today, we know this type of architecture as the common duplex, but at that time, it was new to the community and demonstrated Dow's ability as an inventor in addition to an architect. Work

The W.L. Dow House was a modest Queen Anne with very little ornamentation located on Prospect Hill. Dow lived there with his wife and three children before building a new home on the same land. *Siouxland Heritage Museums.*

The Dow Duplex was constructed in 1900 and was considered one of the first duplexes in Sioux Falls. His son Edwin and his family lived in the southern half, while Wallace and his wife, Lois, lived in the northern portion. By this time, Edwin was a partner with Dow, and the two men's design for the duplex reflected a Tudor Revival style. *Siouxland Heritage Museums.*

started on the Dow Duplex in 1895, but it wasn't complete until 1900. Located next to his original Queen Anne home, this structure reflected a unique Tudor Revival style. W.L. Dow and his wife, Lois, lived in the northern half, while Edwin and his family lived in the southern half. Dow did add a few stylistic features to the home, such as built-in buffets, marble-mantled fireplaces and stained-glass windows, but it was mostly known for its purpose rather than design.

Chapter 10

WORSHIP

Dow had left his mark on downtown Sioux Falls and helped create some of the most elaborate residential homes in the area; however, his legacy for building churches was not as impressive even though no one would argue the vital role religion played in shaping communities. At the time, churches were not only a place to worship but also to meet new citizens. Oftentimes, new pioneers sought refuge and found comfort in finding an appropriate church that simulated that of their homeland. Dow was commissioned to design two churches for Sioux Falls in addition to churches in the surrounding communities of Bismarck, Dell Rapids and Vermillion.

One would easily say the First Baptist Church in Sioux Falls was not a large paying commission for Dow but rather an obligation he owed to his wife, a staunch and active Baptist. Dating back to 1872, the first Baptist services in Sioux Falls were held sporadically due to the small number to form a congregation. Finally reaching a mere eleven members in 1875, Reverend Amos Hilton organized the first official Baptist congregation in Sioux Falls. By 1882, the need for an actual church arose. Lois Dow, having just arrived in Sioux Falls, quickly found solace in the Baptist organization, and the Dow family became members. She didn't waste any time offering up her husband's services to construct a grand church located on the northeast corner of Eighth Street and Dakota Avenue.

So the premier architect of Dakota Territory and member of the congregation designed the elaborate structure. The church was a fifty-five-by forty-nine-foot building with seating for three hundred, even though the

The First Baptist Church was designed by Dow in 1884 and featured a warm-water baptistery, large bell tower, ornamental windows and multiplaned rooflines. Dow and his family were also active members of the church. *Siouxland Heritage Museums.*

congregation was only twenty-five at the time. Dow included innovations such as a warm-water baptistery, making outdoor immersion baptism in the Big Sioux River a thing of the past. The exterior boasted a large bell tower, ornamental windows and multiplaned rooflines. That next year,

Evan Meredith was ordained as pastor, the same man who co-founded the University of Sioux Falls. At the time, Dow surely didn't realize he would later construct a grand fortress named after him. The congregation grew over the years, and new churches were needed to house the additional members. The First Baptist Church was eventually razed.

Similar to the First Baptist Church, Dow was also commissioned in 1884 to build the First Presbyterian Church located on Ninth Street and Minnesota Avenue. The newly formed church held its first meetings in the basement of the First Methodist Church until its own structure was eventually built. At the time, Reverend W.S. Peterson, a Presbyterian missionary, presided over the eighteen-member meetings. By 1884, numbers had increased enough to where a decision to purchase land for the first permanent home of the new church was agreed upon. Having just completed the First Baptist Church, Dow was hired to build a similar structure that was described as being a "fine little church" even though its location next to a barnyard made for noisy clatter during times of solemn prayer. Despite this, the congregation found humor in their additional "members" and were happy to have their own church. The First Presbyterian Church also included a large bell tower, but unlike the First Baptist Church, the exterior had less ornamentation. By 1912, escalating members outgrew the fine little church next to the barnyard, and a series of larger churches was eventually constructed. However, respects must be paid to the original church and its members as being a vital part in the thriving Presbyterian community today.

Chapter 11

Shaping Communities

Southern Towns

While the up-and-coming Sioux Falls relished in being home of the State Penitentiary and kept Dow busy with large commissions, smaller communities throughout the territory would also seek the esteemed architect for similar intentions. Towns like Vermillion and Yankton also sought out settlers and commissioned the resident architect to erect numerous projects to help put them on the map. Even though most of Dow's work was located in Sioux Falls, he had no qualms about helping outside communities with projects. Upon his first arrival in Yankton back in 1880, Dow even kept his original office there after moving to Sioux Falls, where he opened his main office in the Van Eps Block.

In fact, one of Dow's most credited creations was the 1882 design for Old Main on the campus of the University of Dakota in Vermillion. Located in the southeastern corner of Dakota Territory just below the bluffs of the Missouri River, Vermillion was home to various Native American tribes. The name Vermillion stands for the Lakota name *wa sa wak pa'la*, which means red stream. Opened to homesteaders in 1860, the little town was growing and thriving until a major setback occurred in 1881. A great flood washed away three-quarters of the town. But like in Sioux Falls, settlers weathered the hardships, and the town soon flourished and became home to one of the most notable universities in the territory.

Since the 1880s first modest public schoolhouse, the territory was making significant advances and had established five institutions for higher learning. Dow and his rival architect Schwartz would go on to construct more college buildings than any other architects. One of the most significant universities for Wallace Dow would be the University of Dakota in Vermillion.

But the quest for a university was slow for the town of Vermillion. In 1862, it all started when the first territorial governor, William Jayne, approved a territorial university to be located at Vermillion. It would take nearly twenty years before governor Jeremiah Ordway authorized Dakota Territory to purchase land for the University of Dakota. But there was a stipulation: the purchase of land must come after statehood was achieved. Citizens of Vermillion grew impatient and were unhappy with the agreement. They formed a nonprofit organization called the University of Dakota that would eventually gain status as a corporation from the territorial government. The next year, the committee strong-armed a vote that forced approval of a bond to acquire land. In 1882, the committee commissioned W.L. Dow to construct a two-story quartzite building on the newly purchased prairie land northeast of Vermillion. It would serve as the location for the university's first campus building, Old Main.

Most early colleges began with the construction of a building called Old Main, which was a large, multipurpose building that housed both classrooms and a dormitory. "Old Main" is a term used nationwide on college or university campuses. These buildings were also a focal point of the institution and common location for students in the community. Most Old Mains were identified as having a large tower and a cupola or spire that included a bell. Dow took to this national trend when designing Old Main for the University of Dakota in Vermillion. Like most of his buildings in Sioux Falls, the city of Vermillion also wanted to design a grand structure to attract attention and potential students through architecture.

Dow's creation of Old Main for the University of Dakota in Vermillion certainly didn't disappoint. Plans for a grand quartzite design in an eye-catching Venetian/Victorian Gothic style provided a landmark for both the university and city of Vermillion. Before 1883 ended, the university officially moved from its loaned space in downtown Vermillion to the grand structure. With a symmetrical composition, Old Main was built in three sections, west to east, over a five-year period. The university grew slowly but steadily, and appropriations were eventually made to build additional sections of Old Main.

In 1882, a committee in the town of Vermillion commissioned Dow to construct a two-story quartzite building that would serve as the location for the university's first campus building. The grand creation Dow delivered was called Old Main and stood proudly on the campus of the University of Dakota in Vermillion. *Archives and Special Collections, University of South Dakota.*

Just as work commenced on Old Main, Dow immediately began designing the East Hall. Located southeast of the main structure, the girls' dormitory was the perfect companion to Old Main. Built of pink quartzite in a grand Romanesque style, the building featured thick stone walls and round-headed arches above doors and windows. The elaborate structure housed thirty-six girls and was the third building on the campus. The second building, the Armory, was awarded to Joseph Schwartz.

As the university thrived, tragedy struck in 1893 when a fire completely destroyed Old Main. Dow was called upon to construct a new building and was quite anxious to demonstrate the changing trends in design with this new commission. Dow chose to rebuild Old Main using a Georgian Revival–style motif with much less vertical orientation yet continuing to lend itself to the symmetrical façade that had characterized the original Old Main. The style also reflected another building that Dow created: the South Dakota Pavilion for the 1892 World's Columbian Exposition.

Above: The South Dakota Pavilion for the 1892 World's Columbian Exposition in Chicago, Illinois, gave Dow a chance to showcase his talents. The building was a unique Neoclassical design and was composed of only native materials. *Siouxland Heritage Museums.*

Opposite, top: East Hall on the campus of the University of Dakota in Vermillion was located next to Old Main and also featured elaborate detailing and a quartzite exterior. Its initial use was for a girls' dormitory. *Archives and Special Collections, University of South Dakota.*

Opposite, middle: The pairing of Old Main and East Hall took place over the course of five years as the university grew slowly but steadily. To keep up with the growing university, additional sections were eventually added to Old Main. *Archives and Special Collections, University of South Dakota.*

Opposite, bottom: Tragedy struck in 1893 when a fire completely destroyed Old Main. Dow was quickly commissioned to construct a new Old Main. Although it was located in the same place, Dow utilized a different design to reflect the changing times. *Archives and Special Collections, University of South Dakota.*

The 1892 World's Columbian Exposition was a celebration of the 400th anniversary of Christopher Columbus's landing in America. Held in Chicago, Illinois, the fair was a cultural event that was considered highly influential to society. Its architecture and arts were showcases of American industrial optimism. The fair covered more than six hundred acres and featured two hundred buildings from all over the world. Although the structures were temporary, each state took great pride in displaying its grandest forms of building materials and styles. Most structures were Neoclassical and represented cultures from around the world. More than twenty-seven million people attended the exposition, which ran for six months. The selection of Dow as architect was a true reflection of the pride and confidence the community had in his work.

The South Dakota Pavilion was a unique Neoclassical structure with a grand pavilion boasting a full-height semicircular porch, a dominant feature of this type of design. The exterior was finished with Portland cement, also known as Yankton cement, with accents of Sioux quartzite for a perfect contrast. It's said that this building first introduced South Dakota to Neoclassical-style designs, which was later reflected in residential homes. The South Dakota Pavilion was a success, and Dow took home a blue ribbon for his creation.

The pavilion not only introduced a new design but also provided a rare opportunity to advertise the up-and-coming Portland cement found in Yankton, where there was an abundance of chalk rock. Prospectors tapped into the natural resource as an inexpensive building material. Joseph Aspdin, an English bricklayer, patented Portland cement in 1824. The English took to the abundance of rock and opened up a large cement plant four miles west of Yankton in 1890. Called the Western Portland Cement Plant, it processed the Yankton chalkstone with Pierre shale using a semi-wet combination that included clay. Unlike quartzite, which required quarrying and stonecutting, this process was much different. The plant produced the product in droves, giving Yankton the name "Cement City," as it had the largest plant in the United States at the time.

As the grand pavilion was taken apart, Dow utilized the intricate stone blocks in his plans for the second Old Main at the University of Dakota in Vermillion—an ingenious way to honor the award-winning legacy of the pavilion through repurposing for another landmark building. At the University of Dakota in Vermillion, classes would resume in 1895 despite the fact that construction was still underway. Finally, in 1899, the building was complete when the grand towers were added. But over the years, the interior would succumb to deterioration, and in 1973, it could no longer be used as an academic building. The community rallied once again in 1991 to obtain a grant to restore the structure. Final restoration was complete in 1997, and the community celebrated its listing on the National Register of Historic Places with a formal rededication ceremony.

In addition to Dow's contributions to higher learning in Vermillion, he's also credited with designing the Vermillion High School in 1882. While his love for quartzite was ever prominent, he chose to sway from his mainstay

Workers in Vermillion quickly began rebuilding Old Main on the University of Dakota in Vermillion campus after fire claimed the initial structure in 1892. *Archives and Special Collections, University of South Dakota.*

and utilized pressed brick from Yankton to veneer the school. As with Sioux quartzite and Yankton cement, attempts to produce pressed brick in Dakota Territory had been a growing industry. One of the earliest brick plants started in Vermillion in 1861. But it would take years for bricks to be manufactured on a commercial level.

For the Vermillion High School, Dow chose to use bricks produced in the Yankton brickyard. The early operation, which opened in 1868, originally shaped the bricks by hand and placed them in molds to dry before being fired in a kiln. Crude as they were, they were given the name "common brick" because of their soft and porous composition. Eventually, other brickyards would open in both Vermillion and Sioux Falls. W.G. Bower in Vermillion ran one of the most successful brickyards, in business from 1870 to 1905. Meanwhile, Sioux Falls ran a much larger operation. It's said that the Sioux Falls brickyard produced thirty thousand bricks over the course of just one summer in 1873. Later, Dow would utilize many of these bricks for his numerous commissions.

Like Sioux Falls, places of worship were a necessity for the growing and thriving community of Vermillion. Having done a handful of churches in Sioux Falls, such as the First Baptist Church, Dow was hired to construct the First Baptist Church in Vermillion.

In 1872, the original First Baptist Church was a modest wooden building with Gothic elements. After the flood of 1881, it was moved to higher ground until it was razed in 1889 to build the "second" First Baptist Church. Although it was the second time around for the Vermillion Baptist congregation, Dow didn't hold back when it came to introducing new design elements. For the second church, he chose to utilize his famed quartzite Romanesque design. However, Dow did pay tribute to the original church by replicating the crenellated Gothic-style parapet of the 1872 church.

Located not far from Vermillion, Yankton not only produced building products used throughout the territory but was also known as one of the most historic cities in the West. Dow even chose Yankton to begin his practice in 1880. Yankton was opened for settlement by treaty in 1859. The city grew as a stop for steamboats and was the territory capital from 1861 to 1883 before it was moved to Bismarck. In 1873, the arrival of the Dakota Southern Railroad brought an end to the riverboat era, yet the city continued to flourish. By 1879, the city was given appropriations to build the territory's first psychiatric hospital, called the Dakota Territory Hospital for the Insane. Proving there was a great need for such an institution, Wallace Dow was commissioned in 1882 to create a much larger facility. Dow's forward-thinking design schematic for the large campus would be his successful follow-up commission to the Dakota Territorial Penitentiary in Sioux Falls.

In 1903, the town of Yankton was awarded a grant to construct a Carnegie library. The library system in Yankton was first established in 1868 and was called the Yankton Community Library. It was the oldest public library in Dakota Territory. Yankton wasn't the only city to receive the funding; architects other than Dow were constructing libraries in Aberdeen and Sioux Falls. But Dow received the commission for Yankton and built a unique structure out of pressed brick that featured a dome on top. In the 1940s, the dome caved in and was immediately repaired before it was removed altogether later on. There was a much better fate for the building; it went on to serve as the community library until 1972. After that, a number of businesses occupied the space. The building was listed on the National Register of Historic Places in 1979, and today it is used as the Lewis and Clark Mental Health Center.

Western Towns

Sioux Falls served as a central hub for Dow and his thriving business and the southern towns of Yankton, Vermillion and Huron provided some of the most historic opportunities for his design, but he also traveled west to serve similar budding communities looking to acquire significant structures. Located along the James River, the town of Mitchell was incorporated in 1881 and was named after Milwaukee banker Alexander Mitchell, who served as president of the Chicago, Milwaukee and St. Paul Railroad.

A thriving community with a promising future, the city of Mitchell would also be a recipient of grant funding for a Carnegie library in 1904. Dow was commissioned to execute the funds by designing a grand Neoclassical Revival quartzite structure. Construction for the Mitchell Public Carnegie Library started in 1902, and it is architecturally significant as a monument to the skilled stonemasons, woodworkers, glass artisans and ornamental craftsmen of the period. An ornate grill divides the lobby and the former library stack room. This detailing extends into the two side wing rooms above a red brick fireplace and doorways. Later, panels of stained-glass diamonds in hues of gold and purple were added to accentuate the large dome and walkway area. Unlike that of the Yankton Carnegie Library, this dome remained intact and was even a focal point for the building. In 1940, Oscar Howe was commissioned to paint a mural on the dome. It was this act of artistic influence that saved the building from being razed after the library moved out in 1972, despite the fact that an addition had been built for expansion in 1960.

Howe, a famous Yanktonai Nakota Sioux artist, painted the mural called *Sun and Rain Clouds Over Hills* in the Mitchell Public Carnegie Library dome. A South Dakota native, Howe was an esteemed artist whose forty-year art career would win him numerous awards, including grand and first prizes. His art can be seen all over the world in places such as Paris and London. In 2006, the Mitchell Area Historical Society acquired the historic library and currently is working with the Mitchell Area Genealogical Society to preserve the building and its history. Although no longer a public library, the center houses rotating and permanent historic Mitchell exhibits.

Education proved more than vital to Mitchell, as seen in the need for higher learning. In 1883, a group of Methodist settlers in Dakota Territory received a charter to build a college. Called Dakota University, the driven pioneers held deep religious views about education and the future of the community's children. With a growing population of students, the college commissioned W.L. Dow & Son in 1899 to design the New Century Hall. It was the college's second building and was constructed to make room for the growing campus after a fire claimed another structure fourteen years earlier. Later known as Graham Hall, it was said to have been one of the finest buildings of its kind west of Chicago. Known for its modern details, the construction was entirely fireproof and well proportioned with an architectural effect that is enticing and attractive. At a cost of $75,000, the building was considered money well spent to accommodate the growing demands. Over the years, the college would undergo significant changes. In 1904, the college was renamed Dakota Wesleyan University after the Wesleyan Church and Century Hall was renamed Graham Hall in honor of university president William I. Graham, a catalyst for the building's construction.

A town that saw great expansion during the Great Dakota Boom was the new town of Pierre. It began as a ferry landing and was the site of a railroad terminal. The same hardships early pioneers in Sioux Falls faced were also hitting the early citizens of this small town. But like the rest of Dakota Territory, persistence and determination would eventually win out and the town would recover. After many years, the town was awarded

W.L. Dow & Son designed the Pierre Carnegie Library in 1905. The structure included native cut-granite boulders with large white columns in the front. *Siouxland Heritage Museums.*

$10,000 in 1903 as seed money to build another Carnegie library. W.L. Dow & Son began construction of the Pierre Carnegie Library using native cut-granite boulders with large white columns in front. In 1905, the library was officially opened to the public, and it would flourish for the next forty years.

Railroads had proven to be instrumental in the creation of many towns. One town directly linked to the Chicago and Northwestern Railway was Huron. The Great Dakota Boom of the 1880s along with the railroad gave Huron its start. Located on the west bank of the James River, Huron was named after the Huron Indians. Like most small towns surrounding Sioux Falls, Dow would leave his stamp on the small city through architecture. In 1886, M.F. Wright moved to Huron and opened the Wright Hotel. He would later employ Dow to design his commercial block called Wright's Block.

Taking the reins of a family business was quite common in the 1800s. So when Fred, Edgar and Willis Nash took over their father's general store at an early age, they brought with them unique visions and a high value for customer appreciation. Simply called the Nash Brothers Store, they ran a wholesale fruit business that would bring new produce varieties to the Dakota Territory. True entrepreneurs, the Nash brothers also believed in fair prices and built a strong reputation in the area. Dow built the Nash Brothers Store in Huron, and the brothers went on to form the Nash Brothers Trading Company, which supplies goods to numerous local grocery stores even today.

Northern Towns

The quarry industry may have run deep in Sioux Falls, but it helped define the small town of Dell Rapids due to its rich veins of red quartzite that ran 2,600 deep for hundreds of miles. Named for the quartzite dells of the Big Sioux River, where it was located, Dell Rapids was settled in 1871. Quartzite was ever prosperous for the city. Even the downtown architecture of Dell Rapids was inspired by the outcroppings of quartzite and the century-old quarry industry. Stonecutters from England, Scotland and Scandinavia flocked to the quarry towns like Sioux Falls and Dell Rapids. In 1887, the stonecutters organized a union when they realized the industry was established, and a workers' cooperative quarry began in Dell Rapids.

Quarrying of the unique red quartzite in Dell Rapids goes back 120 years, and for the last 80 years, the L.G. Everist Quarry has been a prominent business for the city. Like Sioux Falls, the city of Dell Rapids wanted to make a statement with architecture and selected the use of its native quartzite as the preferred building material. Having worked with quartzite since the onset of his career, Dow was a logical choice when it came to building grand structures of stone. One of his commissions was St. Peter's Lutheran Church. In 1887, Reverend E.H. Midtboe first organized the congregation, which held its early services in the homes of its members. Finally, in 1893, a charter was granted to purchase a lot, but it would be many years before the construction would begin. In 1900, Dow was given the go-ahead, and the building began. The church was completed and ready for worship in 1902. St. Peter's Lutheran Church was one of the first churches to be designed by an architect. Prior to this, the Lutherans believed that churches should be small and modest and resisted spending the money for costly architects. Dow went on to build a grand quartzite church that featured a large single tower and stained-glass windows. It has stood the test of time and is still in use today.

Not only was quartzite a logical building material for its abundance, but it also proved vital for its strength. In 1873, the first educational institution was established in Dell Rapids. Years later, a shanty wood-framed building was constructed and would serve students for nearly a decade until a terrible windstorm completely leveled it in 1884. By this time, the booming quartzite industry combined with the skills of Wallace Dow gave way to a much grander and sturdier stone schoolhouse that later featured an impressive front addition by master stonecutters. After serving the community for nearly a century, the Dell Rapids Schoolhouse was razed in 1982. Although it was considered a loss of historic architecture, at least it proved that even the most devastating windstorms could not level the little stone schoolhouse.

In 1888, a fire proved devastating to numerous commercial buildings. Despite the destruction, the event allowed new construction to feature quartzite. At the time, Dow had designed more quartzite buildings than any other and was about to make an architectural statement using native stone for Dell Rapids. He also chose the Victorian Romanesque design to help boost the business district by giving it a sense of strength and showcasing the dedication the community had in promoting its most profitable resources. One of Dow's most famous post-fire projects was the Grand Opera House.

After the fire, residents realized an opportunity to voice their need for an opera house. With the help of John Adam Cooley, a respected businessman, and M.R. Kenefick, a lawyer and former Dell Rapids mayor, town officials heard the public outcry and granted their wish by announcing the construction of a two-story opera house that could seat up to 450 people. The Romanesque Revival building features classic elements such as round-topped windows, a decorative stepped cornice and large entrance doors. Located on Fourth Street in downtown Dell Rapids, "The Grand," as it's called today, was listed on the National Register of Historic Places in 1978 and is part of the Dell Rapids Downtown Historic District.

Also part of the Dell Rapids Downtown Historic District are the Augustine-Johnson Block, the First National Bank Building, the Cooley Block and the Union Block. The Augustine-Johnson Block is a two-story quartzite-faced building that features a decorative cornice and two storefronts. Similar is the Cooley Block, also located on Fourth Street. Commissioned by J.A. Cooley, the Cooley Block was also a two-story quartzite-faced building but featured a decorative cornice and round-headed and flat-headed windows. Cooley, a respected businessman in Dell Rapids, was also a catalyst in the construction of the Grand Opera House. Meanwhile, the First National Bank Building is one of Dow's more intricate stone creations. It bore prominent architectural features with its castle-like crenellated towers.

The two-story Augustine-Johnson Block in Dell Rapids, South Dakota, has a quartzite rock face and is part of the Dell Rapids Downtown Historic District. *Bill Hoskins.*

Also listed on the National Register of Historic Places is the William G. Milne House, located on Ninth Street. W.L. Dow & Son was commissioned by Milne for his personal home. Dow chose to use the classic Queen Anne design and incorporated a large wraparound porch and small turret. It would later be known as the Norgaard House and the Peterson House.

In the late nineteenth and early twentieth centuries, an adult educational movement swept through the United States. It was called the Chautauqua movement, named after Chautauqua Lake in New York, where the first assembly was held. Eventually, the movement spread throughout the United States and reached South Dakota, bringing entertainment and culture through musicians, entertainers, speakers and even preachers. In the 1880s and 1890s, Chautauqua pavilions were built in numerous South Dakota towns. Although most buildings resembled a tent, some parks featured more elaborate buildings.

In 1891, the South Dakota town of Madison held its first Chautauqua, which would run until 1933. Like the others, the main building was a large tent-like pavilion. But for the guests, the Lake Madison Chautauqua Association enlisted the services of Dow to construct the Grand View Hotel. The famous Chautauqua assemblies often drew in as many as ten thousand people a season and were vital to the development of the town. Madison, which was established in Dakota Territory by William Lee and Charles Walker in 1870, is located on the southwest side of Lake Madison. Both lake and town were named after another city: Madison, Wisconsin, the homeland of both Lee and Walker. Known as a progressive town rich in culture, it was a likely choice for the Chautauqua. When Dow was commissioned to build the Grand View Hotel, it was to provide elegant living accommodations for Chautauqua visitors. The large structure featured double wraparound porches, dormer windows and a small turret. A landmark for the lake, it would serve the thousands who flocked to summertime festivals until it was destroyed by fire a decade after the Chautauqua ended.

In addition to entertainment, Madison was also known as a city that took great pride in education. It was home to the first school in Dakota Territory to offer education for teacher preparation. In 1881, C.B. Kenney, a local representative to the territorial legislature, successfully secured 160 acres of land one mile east of Madison for the new Dakota Normal School. However, the site was considered too far away, so Kennedy offered 20 acres of land on the north edge of Madison. But it came with a stipulation: if the land were ever used for anything other than the original intent, it would be forfeited.

The school started out small; only a few students were enrolled, and classes were held in public buildings until 1883, when plans were laid out for the first campus structure. By 1886, the school was achieving success, and winter term began with over one hundred students. However, a setback occurred when a fire on February 4 completely destroyed the wood-framed structure currently being used.

With help from the city, its citizens and the state legislature, plans immediately were underway to construct a new Normal building, which was named West Wing. Having successfully completed a number of commissions throughout the territory, including the All Saints School in Sioux Falls, Wallace Dow was called upon to supply the design. Located in the exact same location as the previous building, the plans stipulated that Dell Rapids granite, Milwaukee pressed brick and LaCrosse white-cut stone would be used. The seventy-six-foot by eighty-four-foot building housed four levels, including a basement. The interior would feature oak and Georgia pine with a grand central carved staircase leading from the first floor to the third. It was also noted that the building utilized a Haxtan Heating System and housed the university library and the president's office.

In 1904, the second phase of the original plan was completed using the same materials to match the West Wing, called East Hall or Ladies Hall. The two twin buildings would meet very different fates. Over the years, West Wing was carefully maintained. In 1935, a roof was put on, and in 1952, a full renovation took place, making it both modern and fire-resistant. In 1970, the building's name was changed to Beadle Hall in honor of General William Henry Harrison Beadle, the college's third president, and the university's name was also changed to Dakota State University. East Hall, unlike Beadle Hall, was torn down because of deterioration. The connecting phase between the two structures was never complete. Today, Beadle Hall stands as a tribute of unique architecture and is the oldest building in South Dakota still used for its original purpose.

One of the oldest settled towns in Dakota Territory other than Sioux Falls was the city of Flandreau. Settled the same year as Sioux Falls, in 1857, the town was named for U.S. Indian agent Charles E. Flandreau. Quite common during that time, the small town was abandoned within a year due to threatening activities. Just over a decade later, a mere twenty-five families would resettle the town, and it resumed until 1872. It was eventually made the county seat. A famous relative of one of the pioneering families would lead to the establishment of an Indian school. R.F. Pettigrew included the school as part of his successful campaign for U.S. Senate in 1889.

Since 1871, the Flandreau Indian School had been in operation. But a need for a boarding school was ever apparent. An original appropriation of $72,000 in 1892 for the purchase of land provided the location for the first three structures of the boarding school. The close relationship between Dow and Pettigrew was apparent when constructing the buildings, as Dow was enlisted to provide the plans. By 1893, the school was open under the name of the Riggs Institute and was the first boarding school in the United States. One of the first buildings designed by Dow was a classroom building. The large structure was void of any ornamentation but did bear a bell tower to reflect its use.

The name Riggs Institute was in memory of Reverend Stephen Return Riggs. Together with Dr. Thomas S. Williamson, he spent forty years converting the Dakotah language to the written word. This act of long-term dedication gave the Santee, Sioux and other Dakotah-speaking people the opportunity to communicate. The school would eventually be renamed several times over the years, yet its dedication to serving the educational needs of Flandreau children remains.

After statehood was achieved in 1889, many towns vied for the status of state capital. One of those cities was a small town called Watertown located north of Sioux Falls. Founded in 1879, its name is not related to any rivers but rather was named after Watertown, New York, the hometown of the city's founders, John E. Kemp and Oscar P. Kemp. The location of Watertown can actually be credited to the Chicago and Northwestern Railroad and a line that ran to Lake Kampeska. Like in Sioux Falls, the 1880s was a boom decade for Watertown. Town leaders soon sought the talents of Dow to construct a grand city block unlike any other. To demonstrate the city's prominence due to the five railroads that radiated from it, Dow was commissioned to design a large commercial structure in 1887 with the help of John W. Martin.

Martin is given much of the success of creating the prosperous community of Watertown. A professor, he's credited with the establishment of a number of schools and later turned to farming and real estate. He was a driving force for the organization of the Dakota Loan & Trust Company, and Dow would carry through his vision. The massive stone building, which also became known as the Granite Block, was Dow's first large Romanesque-style commercial structure. The quarry-faced masonry massing, contrasting colors, round-arched deep-set voids and overall massiveness made it one of the first substantial buildings of that style in the territory. Over the years, it would serve as a post office, land agency office and bank.

EASTERN TOWNS

Like a blank canvas and an unlimited supply of paint, the city of Pipestone, Minnesota, was another opportunity for Dow to leave his mark. Known for its rich red pipestone and catlinite, a finer-grained quartzite, Pipestone was a mecca for the quarry industry. Dow took advantage of the unique-colored stone in his designs, often coordinating stone from different quarries to get different effects. For example, Dow paired quartzite from Pipestone and Sioux Falls for commissions in Watertown.

Located across the Minnesota border, Pipestone was founded by the inquisitive mind of one man and a poem written by Henry Wadsworth Longfellow. Pipestone was everything and more for Charles Bennet, a druggist from Iowa who was so intrigued by the accounts of the pipestone quarry that he uprooted and traveled to the area. Despite blizzards, fires and droughts, the budding township survived and had acquired twenty-two businesses by 1879. The village was finally incorporated in 1881 and became known for its abundance of stone and unique architecture, most of which Dow played a large part in creating.

In 1898, Dow provided the plans for the First National Bank building. The two-story quartzite building was a true masterpiece for Dow with its decorated gray granite columns and Richardsonian-inspired arches and contrasting stone colors. With a blend of Neoclassical elements, the fluted pilasters with Corinthian capitals support a triangular pediment bearing the

A view of Pipestone, Minnesota, where Dow would take advantage of the rich red pipestone and catlinite as building materials. *Pipestone County Historical Society.*

The First National Bank in Pipestone, Minnesota, was built in 1898. The two-story quartzite building features a blend of Neoclassical elements and Romanesque-style designs. *Pipestone County Historical Society.*

words "First National Bank." But don't let the name fool you; this structure was actually the second home of the First National Bank and was later sold and stripped of its arch, and a good portion of the pilasters were removed during remodeling. Although the building still stands today, the original façade is virtually unrecognizable after having numerous alterations.

Following up his successful commission of the First National Bank, Dow was commissioned to provide the plans for the Ober-Hubbard Building. Located next to the First National Bank on Main Street, the two-story building featured elaborate details such as quartzite dentils, rounded window arches and contrasting-colored quartzite keystones. Stone was brought in from Jasper to create a frieze to border the top and bottom. Completed in 1899, the building originally housed E.W. Crosby's shoe store and D.W. Smith's jewelry store, while the second story was used for offices. In 1910, Max Menzel purchased the structure for his drugstore business, which he would operate for thirty-four years. Later, an aluminum storefront was added to the lower façade and the building was converted into apartments. Despite the change of appearance, the building became part of the downtown historic district and has been listed on the National Register of Historic Places.

The grandest of Dow's commissions in Pipestone, Minnesota, was city hall in 1896. With a mere seven months to complete at a cost of $7,822, the grand structure would serve as another one of Dow's famed quartzite Richardsonian Romanesque designs. Notable for its style, the three-story building features typical Romanesque features such as round-arched windows, a bell tower, heavily rusticated lintels, stone coping gables and finials and a saddleback roof. It originally housed the fire department and numerous local government offices. For over six decades, the city hall proudly served its purpose despite having the bell tower removed due to instability of the roof. In 1966, the city turned the structure over to the Pipestone County Historical Society, under whose supervision it underwent an extensive renovation to become open to the public as the Pipestone County Museum. Today, the symbol of pride in Pipestone still stands on Hiawatha Avenue and serves as a hub for providing historical resources, rotating exhibits and historical and genealogical research and publications.

Chapter 12
COURTHOUSE CRAZE

Rivalry among towns to be the county seat was ever prominent following the Great Dakota Boom of the 1880s. Some cities had already been appointed county seat and were outgrowing their oftentimes modest structures, while others were still vying for the title. The prosperity of the Great Dakota Boom in addition to the new developments gave the opportunity to make a statement with these structures. Townships spared no expense and followed in the footsteps of the Minnehaha County Courthouse in Sioux Falls. As that structure still remained the finest example of Richardsonian Romanesque design in the Midwest, others were quick to commission the highly sought-after "courthouse architect" to create equally impressive structures and allowed Dow to select his style of choice. Although none would live up to the grandiose courthouse in Sioux Falls, Dow did create elaborate buildings throughout the state.

At the same time Dow was designing the famed Sioux Falls structure, a resolution to build the Kingsbury County Courthouse was first introduced. Although initiation of the plans would not begin until 1898, Dow designed the building, which was constructed by M.E. Bush at a cost of $14,800. Utilizing an Italianate influence with red pressed brick, Dow's impressive structure provided a landmark for the newly appointed county seat in the town of De Smet, South Dakota. Dow was also asked to provide plans for an addition, for which he chose to employ a Georgian Revival–style T-plan. It was during this phase of construction that Dow added the famed cupola. In the 1980s, the building was renovated and placed on the National Register of Historic Places.

The small town of De Smet, named after nineteenth-century missionary Pierre De Smet, is located in central South Dakota. Despite the classic courthouse and the town's founding father, it was a famous family who arrived on horse and buggy in 1879 that put De Smet on the map as a tourist attraction. The story of the Ingalls family, as told in the five classic book series starting with *Little House on the Prairie*, was based on the life and experiences of a young girl named Laura Ingalls. The books were made into a long-running television series that remains popular today. The Ingalls family would miss witnessing the construction of Dow's creation by a mere four years. In 1894, they moved from De Smet to a farm in Missouri. Dow's masterpiece was completed in 1898.

In 1875, commissioners granted Canton, a small city located twenty miles south of Sioux Falls, as the county seat for the newly formed Lincoln County and quickly approved that a courthouse be constructed. It was built of brick and contained four offices, a courtroom and a jury room. By 1889, the thriving city had outgrown the courthouse, and plans were made to build an addition. The city of Canton commissioned Dow, who was also working on the Minnehaha County Courthouse at the time, to design a Romanesque-style masterpiece that resembled much of the grandeur being built in Sioux Falls.

Rather than building a new structure, the city approved to erect a three-and-a-half-story addition located east of the old courthouse. The addition was completed in 1890. The courthouse utilized native quartzite to reinforce the Richardsonian Romanesque style Dow favored. During the 1890s, it became apparent that the original 1875 structure had once again become inadequate and more space was needed. Canton businessmen went to work to advance construction funds, which would finance tearing down the original courthouse and electing Dow to extend an addition in its place. In 1899, work began on the building, which included adding the iconic clock tower. In the end, the courthouse perfectly blended the two portions that Dow had created. The final plans had a jail in the basement, main-floor offices, a second-story courtroom with a balcony and access to the attic for the jury. Over the years, the courthouse remained the crown jewel for the city of Canton. Today, the building still stands proud, although its exterior looks quite different after the Works Progress Administration (WPA) covered the stone with stucco. The WPA was one of many New Deal programs created by President Franklin D. Roosevelt during the 1930s. The agency went on to be the largest and most ambitious during its time, accounting for numerous projects. Despite the change in appearance, the original vision of

Dow has remained, and the Lincoln County Courthouse continues to serve the growing community.

Unlike the twin Romanesque quartzite courthouses in Minnehaha and Lincoln Counties, Dow took a turn when designing the McCook County Courthouse, located in Salem, South Dakota. Dow had just designed the South Dakota Pavilion for the 1892 World's Columbian Exposition in Chicago when he was commissioned to design this courthouse. Despite the success of his worldly design, Dow chose not to employ details from his famed building but rather utilized a modest blending of Georgian Revival and late Italianate elements. Dow modified the symmetrical T-plan layout when he replaced the typical corner entrances with a front-door placement.

The structure was eye-catching and interesting; in fact, it was almost as interesting as the quest for the county seat itself. Salem residents back in 1882 were so desperate to obtain the title that they resorted to stealing public records from the existing county seat's courthouse in Bridgewater. Thanks to an unlocked door and lack of law enforcement, Salem would win out. By 1884, the county had built a small two-story courthouse on the same site where Dow would later build his structure.

Chapter 13

DOW INVENTS PERFECTION WITH THE HELP OF A MIRACLE

By the 1900s, architects, builders and inventors were beginning to look into fabricating materials to utilize for building. Proving Dow's ability to be forward thinking and adaptable to current trends, he didn't hesitate to begin experimenting with concrete. Two brothers from Iowa would eventually partner with Dow to turn his career from simply architect to inventor. And their names said it all: the Miracle brothers.

Having started in the lumber business in 1898, O.U. Miracle and R.O. Miracle acquired three lumberyards in Iowa in a matter of three years. They were young and ambitious and sold their lumberyards to purchase one large yard in the city of Sioux Falls in the fall of 1900. Originally, they became interested in laying cement sidewalks and soon took their experience to design a machine for concrete blocks.

Meanwhile, Dow continued to design homes, but his taste for stone and timber was beginning to change, as was the practicality of utilizing quarried rock for building purposes when concrete block was gaining in popularity for its looks, strength and, most importantly, price. Although no records indicate how the Miracle brothers and the Dow brothers first met and became business partners, records indicate that in 1902, Orville U. Miracle, Ralph O. Miracle and Wallace L. Dow each were assigned one-third of a patent to create concrete blocks. Their block design contained vertical air cavities, and the blocks were assembled in rows. In 1903, a patent was also filed for the Miracle block, which took the product from being used mostly for foundations to a whole new level. The concrete frenzy soon took over, and forms were created that produced a wide array of rock faces, sizes, shapes and even colors. The concrete was quickly becoming known for its beauty rather than just sturdiness.

That same year, the Miracle Pressed Stone Company first opened its offices in Minneapolis, Minnesota. With two entrepreneurial brothers running the business, it was said they quickly became the largest manufacturers of concrete machinery in the world. President O.U. Miracle and his brother R.O. Miracle, acting as secretary and treasurer, quickly proved to be two young men who were successful in their business ventures.

In 1905, Dow filed a patent on what he called the Perfection Block Machine and formed the Perfection Block Machine Company. The partnership of architectural knowledge and an already thriving concrete business made for instant success as Dow began to incorporate his newly designed blocks into his later commissions. In 1906, Gottlieb Scheurenbrand, who ran a cement factory, employed Dow and his new pressed concrete block to build his personal residence in Mitchell, South Dakota. It was to be one of Dow's first and finest examples of concrete used for beauty and versatility.

But concrete blocks weren't anything new to the United States. Dating back to 1868, the Frear Stone Manufacturing Company in Chicago, Illinois, had begun to patent concrete blocks that were ornate and appropriate as a major building material. Because of the improvements in Portland cement and the bevy of patented machines, the concrete world was revolutionized by the early 1900s. Like the Dows and Miracles, thousands of companies and individual contractors were inventing machines and utilizing the material for the next ten years. For Dow, those ten years would be his last. Having successfully constructed numerous commissions with his Perfection Block Machine, Dow didn't hesitate to turn his back on the quarry industry for building. But the famed Sioux quartzite still had many uses and would carry on as an identifiable product of the Midwest, even though architects like Dow were ready to move on.

The Miracle Pressed Stone Company had its primary plant in Minneapolis; meanwhile, Dow remained in South Dakota, promoting his patent and continuing to build homes and public buildings. He also traveled extensively to trade shows, where he would demonstrate the making of the block. His brother Wilbur continued working alongside Wallace and touted the product in remote locations such as Buenos Aires.

In 1908, Dow and his associates attended the National Association of Cement Users Annual Convention in Buffalo, New York. It was said that their expansive exhibit for the Perfection Block Machine Company of

Left: In 1905, Dow filed a patent on what was called the Perfection Block Machine. The partnership of architectural knowledge and a thriving concrete business made for instant success. *Siouxland Heritage Museums.*

Below: After forming the Perfection Block Machine Company with his brother Wilbur, Dow began to incorporate his newly designed blocks into his later commissions. *Dow Family Collection.*

Minneapolis attracted much attention. The company took over six regular spaces and demonstrated the complete production of the block by having a plant on site for the manufacture of concrete blocks by its power machine. The company boasted that blocks made by this process could withstand 200,000 pounds of pressure and be cured in twenty-four hours in vapor curing kilns. The finished blocks were manufactured before the eyes of the visitors, faced with any material or coloring desired.

By 1910, myriad stone faces were popular but the pressed stone look often prevailed. Dow utilized this versatility for the second Saint Mary's School, which he designed in 1911. Rather than using all rock-faced or all pressed stones, Dow chose to use a combination for the school, which was located on the Rosebud Indian Reservation.

Chapter 14

THE LOSS OF A LEGACY

Working with cement molds would be Dow's last project. On July 6, 1911, local citizens awoke to a startling headline in the newspaper: "Is Claimed by Death." Wallace L. Dow had passed away at an early hour after a brief illness. Retired and in seemingly perfect health, Dow was stricken with apoplexy during the night. Other than a legacy in stone, he left behind his wife, Lois, and their three remaining children: Edwin, Baron and Annie.

Having been a private man, little attention was paid to Dow in the local newspaper during his career. However, the *Daily Argus Leader* printed this tribute to Wallace L. Dow on July 7, 1911:

> *In the death of Wallace L. Dow of this city, which occurred suddenly yesterday, South Dakota loses a citizen who has been worthy in every relation in life, and whose work in the state as an architect will live long.*
>
> *Mr. Dow came to the state thirty years ago when Governor Ordway was governor of the territory, and designed most of the public buildings erected in the early years. The earlier buildings at the state university, at the hospital for the insane, at the normal schools and state penitentiary were all designed by Mr. Dow. The deceased architect did a great amount of work for the late bishop Hare, designing All Saints School, and most of the Indian buildings erected in the state under Bishop Hare's administration.*
>
> *His monuments are thus scattered all over the state. He leaves in addition, the more lasting monument of a useful life well and bravely lived. Quiet, undemonstrative and dependable, he made a record during his thirty years in*

Dakota, and his twenty-seven years in Sioux Falls, which will forever be a matter of pride to his family and friends and an inspiration to younger men now at work making their record for the judgment of the future.

The city would mourn the death of an early pioneer, an inventor, a promoter and, most important, a dreamer. Without his vision, we may never have known the fate of Sioux Falls. Without his vision, we may never have known the personalities of some of our most noteworthy pioneer settlers. Even before his death, Dow's works were victim to the wrecking ball, something that would forever jeopardize his legacy.

Thankfully, resurgence in restoration took place around the turn of the twenty-first century, breathing new life into abandoned or neglected structures both in Sioux Falls and the surrounding communities. With the financial assistance of state and local grants, downtown business districts began to thrive much like they did when they were first built. Other buildings have been retrofitted to accommodate modern needs, and homeowners are taking pride in restoring historical houses.

Despite the tireless efforts of homeowners, the city and even government, the name Wallace Dow was rarely brought back to life; only his buildings remained. But like most artists, Dow's true fame may still lie ahead. New buildings and structures continue to be researched and associated with Dow. The extent of his work will never be known. For now, it's a matter of appreciating what exists, honoring what is gone and dreaming of what might be.

BIBLIOGRAPHY

Bailey, Dana R. *History of Minnehaha County.* Sioux Falls, SD: Brown & Saenger, 1899.

Cement Age: A Magazine Devoted to the Uses of Cement 6 (n.d.).

Cement World 1 (n.d.): 627.

Daily Argus Leader, July 7, 1911.

Erpestad, David, and David Wood. *Building South Dakota: A Historical Survey of the State's Architecture to 1945*. Pierre: South Dakota State Historical Society Press, 1997.

Fanebust, Wayne. *Where the Sioux River Bends*. Freeman, SD: Pine Hill Press, 1984.

Hoover, Herbert T., and John E. Miller. *A New South Dakota History*. Sioux Falls, SD: Pine Hill Press, 2005.

Hoskins, William J., and David Rambow. *19th Century Sioux Falls Through the Lens Photographs of LeRoy T. Butterfield.* Sioux Falls, SD: Pine Hill Press, 2004.

livingnewdeal.berkeley.edu.

Mueller-Brown, Julie. *Wallace Dow: Builder on the Prairie*. Exhibit, Siouxland Heritage Museums, 1981–82.

Odland, Dr. Rick D. *Images of America: Sioux Falls*. Charleston, SC: Arcadia Publishing, 2007.

Official Gazette of the United States Patent Office 116, part 2.

Olson, Gary D., and Erik Olson. *Sioux Falls, South Dakota: A Pictorial History*. Norfolk, VA: Donning Company, 1985.

Planning and Building Services Department of the City of Sioux Falls. *Historic Avenues Sioux Falls, South Dakota*. Sioux Falls, SD, 1983.

Robinson, Doane. *History of South Dakota*. N.p.: B.F. Bowen & Co., 1904.

Schumacher, Bruce R. "W.L. Dow, Architect, Sioux Falls, Dakota: The Story of a Dakota Builder." Independent study, Augustana College, 1977.

www.NPS.gov.

www.wikipedia.org.

INDEX

S

T

U

V

W

Y

ABOUT THE AUTHOR

Author Jennifer Dumke sits in the Law Exchange Block, where views of what is now the Old Courthouse Museum fill the background. Both constructed by Dow, these iconic buildings are still in use today. Rod Evans, owner of Evans Portrait Gallery, owns the Law Exchange Block, and Dow's famous Minnehaha County Courthouse has been transformed into the Old Courthouse Museum. *Evans Portrait Gallery.*

Jennifer Dumke grew up in George, Iowa, a small town located near the South Dakota border. From the beginning, she knew writing would be a part of her life. She attended South Dakota State University and majored in journalism with an emphasis on broadcasting. After graduating in 1997 with a bachelor of science degree, she immediately moved to Sioux Falls, South Dakota, and landed her first job as a television news photographer and reporter for the NBC affiliate KDLT. It was there that she would meet her future husband, Brad. She quickly realized television news was not the path she would stay on and began writing for print. In 2000, Jennifer and Brad were married, and she began freelance writing for a local magazine called *Sioux Falls Woman*. Her interest in writing for print was extended to television scripts and newspaper, magazine and web content. In addition to freelance writing, she began a career in healthcare philanthropy as a PR/marketing specialist in 2007.

Aside from writing, Jennifer and her husband developed an affinity for history. This would eventually meld into her writing career when the couple decided to produce a historical documentary. In 2009, Jennifer and Brad celebrated the birth of their daughter, Kaydence. Her highly anticipated birth was nothing short of a miracle, and they cherish every day they get to spend with her. In 2011, grant funding was provided to finish their historical documentary, which focused on the life and works of Wallace Dow. What started out as a two-person project now had a third. With Kaydence in tow, the trio hit the road and the books to complete their film. In May 2013, *W.L. Dow, Architect* was released and received positive reviews from the community and the Dow family. It went on to be aired on South Dakota Public Television. Jennifer and Brad both view their work as historical contributions to the community and already have plans to continue focusing on interesting subjects to share. Jennifer also serves on local historical boards and hopes to engage younger people with history.